WHAT DOES THE
BIBLE
REALLY
SAY ABOUT
HELL?

The Living Issues Discussion Series

*T*HE LIVING ISSUES DISCUSSION SERIES IS EDITED by Michael A. King and published through 2002 by Pandora Press U.S., the original name of Cascadia Publishing House, then starting in 2003 by Cascadia. Living Issues titles are also sometimes copublished with Herald Press. Pandora Press U.S./Cascadia Publishing House, in consultation with its Editorial Council as well as volume editors and authors, is primarily responsible for content of these studies, which—typically through main text by author and a chapter of affirming and critical evaluations by respondents—address "living issues" likely to benefit from lively and serious discussion.

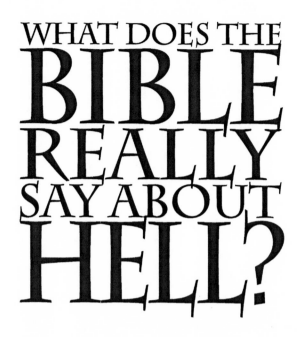

WHAT DOES THE BIBLE REALLY SAY ABOUT HELL?

Wrestling with the Traditional View

Randolph J. Klassen

Foreword by Robert K. Johnston

Living Issues Discussion Series, Volume 2

Pandora Press U.S.
The original name of Cascadia Publishing House
Telford, Pennsylvania

copublished with
Herald Press
Scottdale, Pennsylvania

Pandora Press U.S. orders, information, reprint permissions
Use contact options for Cascadia Publishing House, the new name of Pandora Press U.S.:
contact@CascadiaPublishingHouse.com
1-215-723-9125
126 Klingerman Road, Telford PA 18969
www.CascadiaPublishingHouse.com

What Does the Bible Really Say About Hell?
Copyright © 2001 by Pandora Press U.S., Telford, PA 18969
All rights reserved
Copublished with Herald Press, Scottdale, PA
Library of Congress Catalog Number: 2001044806
ISBN: 1-931038-02-3
Book design by Pandora Press U.S.
Cover design by Merrill R. Miller
Inset cover art by Randy Klassen

Library of Congress Cataloguing-in-Publication Data
Klassen, Randolph J.
    What does the Bible really say about hell? : wrestling with the
    traditional view /
Randolph J. Klassen
        p. cm. -- (Living issues discussion series ; 2)
        Includes bibliographical references.
        ISBN 1-931038-02-3 (trade : alk. paper)
        1. Hell--Biblical teaching. I. Title. II. Series

BS680.H43 K57 2001
236'.25--dc21

                                                          2001044806

        10 09 08 07 06 05   16 15 14 13 12 11 10 9

To my beloved wife, Joyce
who brings me touches of heaven
even while I work on subjects like hell.

Contents

Foreword:
A Theologian of Grace

For his anger is but for a moment;
his favor is for a lifetime. —Psalm 30:5a

I SUSPECT THAT MOST PERSONS PICKING UP this volume have never read a book devoted solely to the topic of hell. It would seem a recipe for depression. But readers of *What Does the Bible Really Say about Hell?* are in for a surprise. Here Randy Klassen is a theologian of grace. In a profound sense, hell is only the pretext of this book; grace is the text. And Randy writes on good authority. His understanding of grace is rooted in Jesus Christ and spelled out in Scripture.

As with all evangelicals, Klassen holds tenaciously to both Jesus and Scripture. But it is important for readers to note Klassen's ordering of these two authorities. He begins Chapter 7 by quoting from an article in *Christianity Today* by Timothy George: "The authority of the gospel is established by the authority of the Bible." Here is a typical Reformed formulation that moves from Word to Spirit, from Bible to the Christian life. But Klassen's theological method reverses this order. Growing up in the Mennonite Brethren Church and ordained as a minister in the Evangelical Covenant Church, he understands that Scripture is first and foremost to be read in the light of the Spirit's witness to Jesus Christ.

Whether Word or Spirit is given epistemological priority is not just a "chicken and egg" argument. The ordering has consequence. Asking questions about a biblical understanding of hell through the eyes of Jesus Christ and his Spirit causes Klassen to turn from focusing on issues of retribution and punishment and to focus, instead, on the good news. The reality of judgment is recognized. But qualifying it and keeping it in perspective is God's amazing grace as revealed in Jesus Christ.

Tellingly, Klassen finds that the early apostolic preaching concerning Jesus recorded in Acts includes no mention of hell. Rather, there is a call to commitment based on the good news of the risen Lord. Klassen finds an underlying gracious intent even in Jesus' language of judgment recorded in the Gospels. Jesus' words must be understood as "siren language," speech meant to cause the hearer to stop, look, and listen. Jesus wants us to repent and experience God's grace.

In this book, the question Klassen asks is, As a Christ-one, a Christian, how can I speak faithfully about hell? How can I formulate a biblically informed perspective on hell "that is morally consistent with the character of God as revealed in Jesus Christ"? If God is not limited even by death, for example, could there be the possibility of a final salvation for all? If the goal of God's justice is closure, not torture, could "annihilationism" be a more biblically consistent doctrine of judgment than eternal torment?

Klassen recognizes the reality of divine judgment but so too "the infinite greatness of God's love." Klassen remains in a questioning mood throughout the text, as any student of Scripture must on this topic. But he is also not without passion. He does not know how to reconcile at every point God's wrath with God's love. There is judgment, and warning is part of the gospel message. But he writes tellingly when he asserts that "It is correct to say, 'God is love'; it is wrong to say, 'God is wrath.' Anger is an action of God, not a fundamental characteristic."

Reading Klassen's book reminded me of an earlier theologian of grace, Dietrich Bonhoeffer. In his *Letters and Papers from Prison,* written from a concentration camp during World War II. Bonhoeffer explored what it would mean to have Jesus in the center of our present life, a Jesus who allowed himself to be pushed out of the world and on to a cross. Writes Bonhoeffer, the God of the Bible "wins power and space in the world by his weakness" (letter of July 16, 1944). One implication for Bonhoeffer of leading a Christ-like life was his rejection of any evangelistic scare-tactics by the church. We should not try, for example, to make room for God by focusing our witness on the ultimate questions of death, guilt, and so on. To concentrate one's attention on those "secrets known to (someone's) valet" to encourage repentance was simply a form of religious blackmail. A Christian apologetic of "sniffing-around-after-people's-sins" was "ignoble," "un-Christian" and, in the end, "pointless" (letter of June 8, 1944).

Klassen would concur. Klassen believes we need not try to scare people into the kingdom with threats of hell as eternal torment. Too much of traditional preaching on hell has sought to win converts through power plays rather than through grace.

Here, in a small book on hell, Klassen offers a wise and helpful perspective on Christian evangelism. What should our witness be like? It should call people to judgment. "But," states Klassen, "grace is greater than judgment. 'Grace that is greater than all our sin,' states the hymn writer." I concur.

Not all will agree with Klassen's hope-motivated conclusion as he suggests the possibility of hell's temporary status. But all will sense his humble spirit and profit from his biblical reflections. Most of all, readers will be encouraged to focus once again on the grace of Jesus Christ, a grace that is not complete until the last sheep is found (Matt. 18) and the lost son comes home (Luke 15).

—*Robert K. Johnston*
  Professor of Theology and Culture
  Fuller Theological Seminary
  Pasadena, California

Series Editor's Preface

*B*ECAUSE THE TOPIC OF HELL IS A "LIVING ISSUE" THAT deserves serious discussion and an examination of various ways Christians understand the topic, *What Does the Bible Really Say About Hell?* seems an appropriate volume to include in the Living Issues Discussion Series. To set the conversation in motion, typically books in the series include a vigorous statement of position regarding an issue or set of issues sometimes controversial in faith circles. Then, after a book's main text, a Responses chapter provides affirming and critical commentary followed by discussion resources.

The result in this case is a stirring book indeed. Author Randy Klassen capably and passionately portrays a God whose judgment remains fearsome yet whose grace must outweigh views of hell as everlasting torment. The conversation between judgment and grace Klassen sets in motion is vividly evoked on the book's cover, which shows superimposed on a medieval portrait of hell the image (painted by Klassen himself) of the loving parent who welcomes home his lost son.

Next respondents Linford Stutzman, Nancy Heisey, Delores Friesen, and Peter Dyck insightfully affirm Klassen's vision and also—as they were asked to do—probe ways in which it, like any one person's perspective, might be enlarged. Then guidelines for discussion as well as discussion questions invite all readers to join Klassen and respondents in learning more about how God may both chasten and love us all.

—*Michael A. King, Living Issues Discussion Series Editor*

Author's Preface

WHY WRITE ABOUT HELL? FOR MANY IT'S A JOKE. It seemed especially funny when the TV news reported snow falling in Hell, Texas—causing hesitation in the use of the phrase "till hell freezes over." In the Phoenix area there is talk of sinners getting some years off their "hell sentence" because of time served in the sweltering summers of southern Arizona. Magazines like the *New Yorker* love to use cartoons which depict the horned devil chatting with surprised arrivals in the fiery region. Hell and the devil have been the butt of many a joke.

For others it is a more serious issue. What does a teaching of hell say about God? Some preachers use fear of hell to keep the flock in line or try to frighten unbelievers into repentance. Some evangelists don't hesitate to use this approach. Many of us after September 11, 2001, are wondering again how to think about God's judgment. But most ministers are avoiding the topic of hell altogether. My uncle Peter, who has preached the gospel for over fifty years, told me he couldn't remember preaching on hell then added, "There are better things to preach about." I couldn't agree more.

So for me to write about hell may seem at first out of character to those who know me. In fact, a member of one congregation I served chided me for not preaching about hell. My reticence reflected, no doubt, a general nervousness among clergy today to preach about hell, so my response to him was admittedly trite. Since I knew some members had to endure a sort of hell all week, I said I would rather give them a good dose of heaven on Sunday! My preference is to follow the example of the Bethlehem angel whose message was, "*good* news of *great* joy for *all* the people" (Luke 2:10, emph. added). To me this is being "ev-*angel*-ical." I want to be that kind of "angel-messenger."

However, the questions of thoughtful people deserve careful answers. When it comes to grieving folks, the need for sensitivity in response is imperative. When asked about the departed loved one, it is certainly appropriate to withhold judgment. Yet the nagging questions remain. What does happen to those who die, especially those who have not passed the litmus test of orthodoxy? Or are there other criteria? Other destinations? What do our answers tell us about God?

While every author hopes his efforts will be widely read, I am most anxious that "Bible-believing" Christians ponder what I have written. I consider myself in this camp. The watchword in the early days of our Evangelical Covenant denomination was, "Where is it written?" This still applies. Sentiment or personal preference must not be determining factors in establishing Christian dogma.

One motivation for writing this material was the discovery that what has often been believed to be the biblical teaching is not, on closer examination, the complete story. I have found that many of the images of hell used in some evangelical preaching actually come from Mesopotamian mythology, the Apocrypha, a misunderstanding of biblical literature, medieval art, or even Hollywood, not from careful biblical exegesis. Where the word *hell* is used in the King James Version it is usually a translation of *Sheol*—the grave, or Hades—the land of the dead. When the word *Gehenna* is used, its reference is to the Valley of Hinnom, which Jesus used as a powerful metaphor for judgment. These simple discoveries led me to study the significant references to hell in the Bible. What I found is contained in this book.

My primary motivation is to share a view of God that is in harmony with Jesus Christ. The living Word of God, Jesus, is our best guide to understanding the inspired written Word of God. Without sliding into sentimentalism, the Christian portrayal of God must not be distorted or corrupted by suggesting that God would sanction a form of punishment so cruel it could only be termed demonic. On the other hand, we cannot disregard those passages that clearly teach a serious judgment for God-rejecters. Yet as those made in the divine image we long for a justice where the punishment fits the crime.

So what view of judgment harmonizes with the love of God as revealed in Jesus Christ? What does the Bible mean by hell? The concepts of personal responsibility and accountability are clearly taught. Judgment day is both every day and a coming day. What happens when creatures appear before the Creator? How do justice and mercy meet on that day? What is the Bible really saying?

Many devout persons far more scholarly than I have pondered these questions throughout the ages. While I hope to add something of substance to this discussion, I would be presumptuous to assert that I can give definitive answers to such questions. What follows is my fallible yet best effort to interpret the meaning of the written Word in harmony with the living Word, Jesus Christ. I trust the reader will then find that even in a book about hell, there is still good news, of great joy, for all the people.

—*Randy Klassen*
  San Andreas, California

Acknowledgments

WITHOUT THE SUGGESTIONS, CONSTRUCTIVE CRITICISMS, and encouragement offered to me by the following persons, this book would not have been written. However, I am not saying that these friends are in full agreement with me about the conclusions of this study. In fact, I was warned by some that I must be prepared for a negative response from many. I appreciated their concern yet remain hopeful of some positive feedback as well.

First I want to pay tribute to my uncle, Peter Dyck, pastor, author, scholar, and one whose major contribution has been directing the Mennonite Central Committee in relief operations and refugee resettlement. Having seen enough of hell in the war-torn areas of Europe he was not necessarily enthused about my topic but provided very helpful guidance.

Reverend Wesley Nelson, well known to the Covenant Church family, is a popular teacher, preacher, and mentor to many of our pastors, including me. His friendship and advice has always been much appreciated, including some ideas for this book.

Dr. Klyne Snodgrass, professor of New Testament Studies at North Park Theological Seminary, gave my first draft a thorough and very helpful critique. This caused me to rewrite much of it, producing, I trust, a more biblically consistent treatment of the subject.

In a similar way, Dr. Robert K. Johnston, professor of Theology and Culture at Fuller Theological Seminary, provided insights for improving the text. His affirmation that "God's YES is always bigger than his NO" became a clinching theme for my book.

One of the hardest workers with the most tedious job was my gracious secretary, Terry Hill. She typed, retyped, and again retyped the manuscript, from my handwritten pages, without a complaint. Always it was done with a smile and the response, "No problem." After our move from Arizona, Gigi Cobb picked up the computer assignment and did it with equal grace. Many thanks, Terry and Gigi.

I also extend a sincere word of thanks to Jeff Warner for editorial assistance with early versions of the manuscript, and to Barbara Robidoux for her most helpful critique of a later draft.

Finally I want to acknowledge the love and support of my wife, Joyce. Her constant reminder to "keep it light" has kept this text from sinking in the sea of theological jargon, wonderful as that may sound to some of us. Thanks for hanging in there with me, Joyce. "Hell" is not normally something married couples want to share. In this instance, Joyce was a constant reminder of heaven.

There are family members and friends I have not named who also provided encouragement in the writing of this book. For their help I am also very grateful, since God has a way of using all of his children to reveal the varied ingredients of his grace.

I am above all grateful for God's presence with me throughout this study. Our Lord knows the intent was to understand God's ways more clearly. God alone knows the degree to which this was achieved. I can testify that my worship of the Savior has deepened. I hope that will also be true for each reader.

WHAT DOES THE
BIBLE
REALLY
SAY ABOUT
HELL?

1

Personal Pilgrimage

Pondering On The Bus

I remember the inner turmoil I felt as I rode home from Pasadena, California, to Winnipeg, Canada, on the Greyhound bus. It was back in 1956 when I was a student at Fuller Theological Seminary preparing for Christian ministry. I thought about all the people coming and going on the bus (my mode of travel in those days). I wondered, were they heaven-bound or hell-bound? The possibility of hell for so many led me to rethink whether I wanted to enter the ministry. If I couldn't believe in hell, perhaps I should find another vocation.

However, my Christian experience had been very real. My encounter with the Lord had been in response to my prayer for cleansing, forgiveness, and a new orientation of caring. God's presence in my life was evident to parents and close friends. I had experienced what we often call "being born again." The fear of hell never entered my mind. I was eager to live in a manner that could merit God's "Well done!"

In the enthusiasm of this first love for my Lord and Savior, I felt called to the ministry. My Intervarsity Christian Fellowship sponsor had recommended Fuller Theological Seminary in Pasadena so that was where I had been studying. Now I was coming home. I had run out of money and had no green card.

As I pondered the possibility of hell for many of my fellow passengers, as well as most people on earth, (at least so it seemed according to my theology at the time) I brought the question to my Lord. I knew Jesus loved all people. I believed he was the key to truth, so what he would say about the subject would settle the matter. Reading through Matthew's Gospel, I discovered that Jesus referred to hell nine times. That settled it for me—hell had to be real. I knew little about biblical hermeneutics (principles of Bible interpretation), less about the biblical languages, and didn't try to resolve the tension between cruelty and grace. I would leave that with my Lord.

Pastoral Questions

I did go into the ministry, not so much to rescue folks from hell as to help people find the grace of pardon and the ability to love each other now in this present needy world. I wanted to assure them of God's love and the availability of this love through the Holy Spirit. I once heard a speaker say, "Even if there wasn't a hell to shun or a heaven to gain, I wouldn't want to live one day without my Savior." My heart warmed to that sentiment. Of course I also felt grateful that my final destination was a place called heaven.

I heard that Jonathan Edwards was a great preacher whose messages brought revival to many in the mid-seventeen hundreds. One of his famous sermons was "Sinners in the Hands of An Angry God." I marveled that it could have been so effective. Fear is a powerful motivator and can be healthy when it keeps us from making destructive decisions. But in a relationship created and sustained by love it seemed out of place. I wasn't about to borrow Edwards' sermon.

As with most pastors, the longer I spent in ministry the more funerals I conducted. Pastors cannot help but think about the destiny of the person whose remains they are committing to the earth. When the individual has lived far short of biblical standards and made no profession of faith, what can we say about that person's final destination? Many of us choose to keep silent. How can any of us really know?

Nels Ferré once said that he could not enjoy heaven if he thought his mother was in hell. I had to agree. I could not even enjoy heaven if I thought my dogs were in hell! Nevertheless, sound theology is not built on emotion.

Harvest Principle

More to the point was the scenario Dr. Edward John Carnell gave his class one day. "What kind of mental balance would you attribute to the university president who welcomes the incoming class with a greeting that included this assurance: 'Whatever you all do is okay. Have a good time. You will all graduate with honors'?"

As students we might like that welcome—for a while. But certainly it would become clear that it does matter what we do with our opportunities. A university president who would say otherwise would be unfit for the position. Are we then to attribute such mental imbalance to God? Those who suggest it doesn't matter how we live, and that it will all be fine in the end, have not reckoned with the fact that freedom and responsibility go together. The One who gave us freedom has every right to expect an accounting of how we used that freedom. Justice demands it.

This logic held me for years. The harvest principle certainly makes sense. When Paul said, "We reap what we sow," he was articulating a principle that operates in the spiritual world as well as in the field of agriculture. But what happens when things don't seem to work out justly on this earth? Heaven and hell seem to be needed to settle all things fairly in the end. Except that fairness or justice may not be well served by either heaven or hell! Each can seem unjust or unfair in either direction! Heaven is better than fair. Should we not then expect hell to be worse than fair? So this harvest principle, which seemed so helpful at first, began later to raise more questions.

Since I had no solutions to the questions I was posing, I was happy to leave them with the Lord, together with the frivolous issues of hell's temperature and architectural details. "Shall not the Judge of all the earth do what is just?"

(Gen. 18:25) Of course! But when we speak of this Judge, this God and Father of Jesus Christ, what are we attributing to our Creator? When we say something about heaven or hell we are also saying something specifically about God. Time and again, during my time of wrestling with this issue, I would be startled by the way some preacher, writer, or evangelist would make references to God sending people to hell. Their approach seemed far removed from anything Jesus would teach, even when he was speaking of hell.

A Hellish Revelation

Mary Baxter's book, called a national best seller, is a case in point. In *A Divine Revelation of Hell* she tells of her visionary journey into hell as led by her Lord so she would know personally how awful a place hell is and thus feel more keenly motivated to save people from it. Her daily visions, for forty nights, convinced her that hell is a "horrid place of torments, excruciating pain, and eternal sorrow."

She goes on to say, "If you are a sinner when you die, you go immediately to a burning hell. Demons with great chains will draw your soul through the gateways of hell, where you will be thrown into pits and tormented."[1] She describes hell as in the shape of a woman's body located in the center of the earth. In closing she states that "the things you have read in this book are true. Hell is a real place of burning torment."[2]

No doubt this writer is sincere. But her descriptions are closer to Hollywood horror films than to biblical revelation. The Jesus she portrays is not the Jesus of the Gospels. Some folks may be scared into the kingdom, but many will be turned off. Her imagination has been fed by a form of preaching that reveals ignorance of both biblical literary forms as well as the historical origins for the cartoonish description she calls a true revelation.

Fear, the Motivator

Baker's imaging of hell must have been the type Madalyn O'Hare had in mind. Before her mysterious disappearnce, this one-time leader of the American Atheist Society claimed Christians "need hell" to keep the church members in line. She went on to say in one of her monthly periodicals, *The American Atheist* that "The fear of hell is the basis for the Christian faith." I was amazed by the comment, until I realized maybe it was true for some Christians. I think of those paintings from the Middle Ages and Dante's "Inferno," and I recognize that fear has its role to play in many lives. We fear certain diseases and take the appropriate healthy precautions.

Clearly, then, hell can be seen as a divine "stop-sign" to cause us to repent, turn around, and go God's way. But is it a sign, a reality, or both? If the lake of fire that burns sinners endlessly is real, what does it say about God? This is the question that has concerned me most.

Recently I read a number of books on the subject of hell, most supporting the traditional orthodox view. I found myself grateful for their arguments, because they led me to examine other views, some of which seemed more defensible than the positions the authors were defending.

On the other hand, books which challenged the traditional view did not always come across as totally convincing either, which illustrates the complexity of the issue. Among the most challenging authors were Alan Bernstein, John Stott, Clark Pinnock, William Crockett, and Jan Bonda, whose recent English translation of his Dutch work, *The One Purpose of God*[3] came to my attention after my first draft of this book was written. I found Bonda's writing most helpful and added some of his insights to this text.

In the chapters to follow I share some of my discoveries. We begin with a survey of first-century preaching. Looking through the book of Acts we examine every message to see if the concept of hell is included, and if it is, what is being said. Surely the preaching of Peter, Stephen, Philip, and Paul as recounted by Luke should tell us much about the themes and emphases of the first Christian preaching. Considering both its nearness in time to the teaching of Jesus and its effectiveness in the world, first-century preaching may be an excellent pattern to follow.

Then we look at the Hebrew Bible, the Scriptures of Jesus, and proceed to the Gospels and the epistles of the apostles. After that we trace the history of the traditional view of hell and ponder its implications for the church today.

Now let's look at those first messages.

2

Apostolic Preaching

*T*HE MESSAGES LUKE RECORDS IN THE BOOK OF ACTS are certainly abridged versions of the original proclamations. However, we must believe that the most memorable and important themes are included. These sermons and testimonies provide us with the basic material that describes first-century preaching. As Richard Longenecker has stated, "It must be insisted that the book of Acts—particularly in its first fifteen chapters—is of major importance for the study of the earliest Christian preaching."[1]

As we listen to what is emphasized, we hear the affirmation that Jesus is Lord. The risen Christ is central to all of the messages. References to passages of the Old Testament figure in many as well. Some are taken literally, some employ a "midrash" interpretation (going deeper than mere literal sense), and a few are even taken allegorically.

The preaching was intended to elicit a decision. That decision was much more than opting to "accept Jesus Christ as personal Savior." It was a call to a new allegiance, a call to embrace the promised Messiah, a call to follow Jesus Christ as Lord!

Peter's Preaching

The first sermon in Acts is Peter's Pentecostal message (Acts 2:14-40). Almost half is quotation from the Scriptures

(Joel and the Psalms primarily) to authenticate the Messiahship of Jesus. Peter wants his Israelite audience to hear that the events they have witnessed were anticipated in their own prophetic writings. The call is to repent, be baptized, receive the gift of pardon and be identified with Jesus Christ and his church. There is no reference to hell.

The call to salvation is not even couched in a promise of heaven. Rather it is an exhortation to "Save yourselves from *this corrupt generation*" (Acts 2:40, emph. added). On that day, about three thousand responded and were added to the community of faith called "the Way" (Acts 9:2, 19:9, 23).

Peter's second sermon once again includes reference to Moses and the prophets. It centers in the risen Christ and credits his power for enabling a lame man to walk again (Acts 3:12-26). The challenge Peter gives is for his hearers to "repent and turn to God." He refers to Jesus as the Messiah who, having risen from the dead, will remain in heaven "until the time of *universal* restoration that God announced long ago" (Acts 3:21, emph. added). This is suggested by his references to the promise made to Abraham that through his descendants "all the families of the earth shall be blessed" (verse 25).

A reference to a rooting out of the people is stated for the disobedient (verse 23), but no reference to hell is made. The purpose of God's Servant-Savior was to "bless you by turning each of you from your wicked ways" (verse 26). Salvation according to Peter has a powerful present effect on the orientation and conduct of people who respond to the lordship of Christ.

Testimonies of Stephen and Philip

The next major message recorded in Acts is Stephen's defense before the high priest and council (Acts 7:2-50). A recital of Old Testament history from Abraham to Solomon, it points out the frequent rejection of God's servants and their messages throughout the ages. He then cites their persecution of him as following this tragic tradition.

Enraged by this charge they drag Stephen out of the city and proceed to stone him to death. This would seem a good time for Stephen to remind his slayers that hell may await them for such cruelty. Instead, his final words are a prayer for the persecutors: "Lord, do not hold this sin against them" (Acts 7:60). This prayer beautifully follows the example of his Lord (Luke 23:34).

The next message in Acts is given by Philip. He meets an Ethiopian eunuch returning from Jerusalem and reading from the book of Isaiah. Philip joins him to help him understand this passage, as quoted in Acts 8:32-33:

> Like a sheep he was led to the slaughter,
> and like a lamb silent before its shearer,
> so he does not open his mouth.
> In his humiliation justice was denied him.
> Who can describe his generation?
> For his life is taken away from the earth.

From this reference Philip proceeds to proclaim "to him the good news about Jesus" (Acts 8:35). The Ethiopian responds with an affirmation of faith, baptism, and rejoicing.

The topic of hell does not come up.

Saul's Conversion

In the record of Saul's conversion, the voice from heaven identified as that of Jesus challenges him with this question: "Saul, Saul, why do you persecute me?" (Acts 9:4). The risen Lord challenges a thoughtful enemy to rethink what he is doing. The persecution of the church is continued persecution of Christ.

The Lord's identity with his suffering people left an indelible impression on Saul, who realized the falseness of his current direction and chose thereafter to follow Christ. This obedience, which characterized the church's greatest first-century missionary, was not brought about by threats of hell. It was an encounter with the living Christ who, although clearly death's conqueror, remains linked to his children with ties of love that feel the pain of their suffering. Moved by such love, Paul later expressed his willingness to suffer for the sake of the church (Col. 1:24).

Peter and Paul

Peter's witness to Cornelius is a powerful message about God's inclusive love (Acts 10:1-48). Not only does it exclude any reference to hell; it makes some of the most powerful affirmations about God's universal love. Peter explains why, contrary to Jewish custom, he is ready to come into a Gentile home. He says, "God has shown me that I should not call anyone profane or unclean" (Acts 10:28). When Cornelius shares with Peter his prayer and its visionary answer to send for him, Peter replies, "I truly understand that God shows no partiality, but in every nation *anyone* who fears him and does what is right is acceptable to him" (Acts 10:35 emph. added). Peter then recites the events of Christ's life and death culminating in his resurrection, thus qualifying Jesus to be the one ordained of God to judge both the living and the dead (Acts 10:42).

Paul's first recorded message (Acts 13:16-41) follows the pattern of Peter and Stephen. He tells the story of Jesus with references to the prophetic Scripture, then proclaims the resurrection as the vindication of Jesus' authority to forgive sins. The good news centers in freedom from the bondage to sin (Acts 13:38, 39). No mention of hell is made, not even after Paul is beaten and stoned. He remains a messenger of good news, not a herald of doom.

The evangelistic adventure in Philippi includes encounters with Lydia, "worshiper of God"; a slave girl; and a Roman jailer and his family (Acts 16:11-34). In each case salvation ensues without threats of ultimate consequences, even after Paul and Silas are unjustly beaten and imprisoned.

A model for evangelistic preaching is presented in Luke's record of Paul's address on Mars Hill. Paul has studied the culture of the people he is addressing. He praises them for their spiritual interest: "I see how extremely religious you are in every way" (Acts 17:22). He starts where they are and chooses their altar, "To an unknown god" as his launching pad. He does not use Hebrew Scriptures in this setting. Recognizing a Greek audience he quotes Greek writers whose messages harmonize with biblical teaching. Referring to the living God, Paul says, "In Him we live and move and have our being; as even some of your own poets have said, for we too are his offspring" (Acts 17:28).

Then Paul does call his hearers to repent. A day of accountability lies ahead. God will judge the world by the one whom he raised from the dead. The resurrected Christ is again at the center of apostolic preaching.

Paul's farewell message to Ephesus church elders is also instructive. He reviews what he has been preaching and the ensuing suffering. The urgency of the good news has motivated him to proclaim what he urges them to preach—"the message of his grace, a message that is able to build up and to give you an inheritance. . ." (Acts 20:32).

In Acts 22-26 Paul defends himself before the tribune in Jerusalem, then Felix, governor of Caesarea, then King Agrippa. In each case he recounts his personal experience of the Damascus Road encounter. The risen Christ turned his life around and he could not do otherwise than proclaim the good news of pardon and hope offered to all people through Christ. These testimonies include his personal call to conversion, his missionary activity, and the theme of all his preaching—the risen Lord Jesus Christ. In none of these testimony presentations is a threat of hell included. This omission is significant in view of the people addressed.

The last two chapters in Acts describe how Paul was taken as a prisoner to Rome aboard a sailing vessel accommodating about 276 (some manuscripts read 76) persons (Acts 27:37). Luke provides us with a detailed account of the sea voyage, the storm, the shipwreck, the hospitality of the natives of Malta, and the eventual arrival in Rome some three months later.

During the height of the storm, when their lives were imperiled, Paul is said to have offered crew and passengers words of hope and assurance (Acts 27:24-26, 33-38). A crisis like this one, with life and death in the balance, might seem an opportune time to challenge all with the prospect of heaven or hell. No hint is given that Paul took this approach. Why he didn't is worth pondering.

Once in Rome, under house arrest, he is allowed visitors with whom he can share the gospel. This he is eager to do, first to the Jews. The message is about Jesus and the Scriptures used are from the law of Moses and the prophets. Some accept the good news. Concerning the rejecters, Paul quotes Isaiah 6:9-10 as predictive of their hardness of heart, but he adds no threat of any literal lake of fire awaiting them. Instead he turns his efforts toward the Gentiles, "proclaiming the kingdom of God and teaching about the Lord Jesus Christ with all boldness and without hindrance" (Acts 28:31).

It is interesting to note an absence of much reference to apostolic preaching in the books that plead the case for eternal punishment. Such is the case in *Hell on Trial,* by Robert A. Peterson. In his whole chapter on the witness of the apostles there is not one reference to any testimony or preaching in the book of Acts.[2] Such is understandable. Hell is absent from the apostolic preaching.

It must be taken seriously that the content of first-century proclamation according to the book of Acts lacks any reference to hell; judgment is addressed, yes, but hell, no. The significance of this omission has been missed by "hellfire and damnation" preachers throughout the centuries. Yet surely the preaching of those first messengers of the gospel, those nearest to the ministry of Jesus, ought to be a reliable model for us. Despite the godless character of their surrounding culture, they never felt the Spirit leading them to use threats of hell in their proclamations.

We need to appreciate the apostles' understanding of judgment and will address this in later chapters, but for now we recognize that their proclamation was the good news focused on the risen Lord. Allegiance to Jesus was the call to commitment. It was not "believe or else you are doomed to hell." "Jesus Christ is Lord" was their living creed. This is still the creed of all true Christians.

3

No Hell in the Hebrew Bible

WHAT WERE THE SOURCES OF FIRST-CENTURY PREACHERS? Their driving motivation and central theme, of course, was their risen Lord. Allegiance to Jesus Christ was their personal commitment as well as evangelistic challenge to others. Following Jesus would make the difference God wanted in people's lives for time and eternity. The Law, Prophets, and Writings (the Hebrew Bible we call the Old Testament) provided the written material undergirding their proclamation. The teachings and actions of Jesus were available through oral sources. These eyewitnesses had not yet inscripturated their testimony; that would soon follow. But during the years covered by Acts, the major written source would be the books of the Hebrew Bible. Some Apocryphal writings were also available but rarely used in first-century Christian preaching.

Let's consider what these early preachers understood from their biblical heritage regarding hell. Thirty-one uses of the word *Sheol* translated "hell" appear in the KJV. (There are altogether sixty-five references to Sheol, but thirty-one are translated "grave" and three times "pit.")

Sheol, Land Of The Dead

The newer translations like the NIV and the NRSV never translate Sheol as hell. However, since many believers still use the KJV. it may be helpful to look at those references. (I will, however, be quoting from the NRSV unless otherwise noted.) A hint of the "netherworld" will appear in some uses of Sheol.

The first such reference is in Deuteronomy 32:22, where in this "Song of Moses" the writer describes God's anger as burning "unto the lowest hell" (KJV) or the "depths of Sheol" in dramatizing the intensity of God's provocation with his people. In 2 Samuel 22:6 David is speaking about his experience of dire distress in these terms: "The cords of Sheol entangled me, the snares of death confronted me." The poetic imagery using synonymous parallelism is fitting to describe betrayal and the threats against his life but makes no reference to an after-this-life venture. In the book of Job there are two references to Sheol (Job 11:8; 26:6). In each case the word is used to describe the wisdom and greatness of God— "higher than heaven, deeper than Sheol," or "Sheol is naked before God."

There are numerous references to Sheol in the Psalms but here again the poet is referring to death and/or the grave (Psalm 9:17, 16:10, 18:5, 55:15, 86:13, 116:3). In 1611 the word *hell* seemed appropriate for translating Sheol, but those who use the King James Version need to understand that this usage in no way supports a teaching of hell as the region of eternal punishment. In fact, in the mind of the Psalmist, God is also present in Sheol, as in Psalm 139:8, where the poet says, "If I ascend to heaven, you are there; if I make my bed in Sheol, you are there." Such is obviously not a reference to hell as the zone of separation from God.

Proverbs usess Sheol in the same way the poets of the Psalms understand it. In Proverbs 5:5, 7:27, 15:11, 23:14, 27:20 the references are clearly to death or the grave. In Proverbs 9:18 we get a hint of the judgment theme, and in 15:24 the ideas of "heaven above," and "hell below" are suggested in these words: "For the wise the path of life leads upward, to avoid Sheol below." Whether this implies something following death is not clarified, although it certainly implies that the unwise are on a dangerous path.

In the poetry of Isaiah, Sheol becomes animated: "Sheol has enlarged its appetite and opened its mouth beyond measure" (Isa. 5:14). "Sheol beneath is stirred up to meet you when you come; it rouses the shades to greet you. . . . Your pomp is brought down to Sheol . . . maggots are the bed beneath you and worms are your covering" (Isa. 14:9-11). "You are brought down to Sheol, to the depths of the Pit" (Isa. 14:15). These references are to the defeat of Babylon, the descent of the arrogant enemy of Israel. In Isaiah 28:15, the image clearly means death and in 57:9 it suggests the farthest reaches of the earth.

Sheol is not used in the closing sections of Isaiah. However, a vision of final judgment is given with images of "fire," "sword," and "undying worms" (Isa. 66:16, 24).

In Ezekiel 31 we encounter an oracle of judgment against Egypt and the nations. Sheol is used in 31:15, 16, 17 to represent the "world below" (31:18) which in this picture even includes "the trees of Eden." As with most of the allegorized writings of Ezekiel, no literal interpretation is intended.

Amos uses Sheol to express an extreme effort of some to escape from the Lord (Amos 9:2). Jonah also uses the term to express extremity, in his case the belly of the fish in which he finds himself (Jonah 2:2).

The last reference to Sheol in the Old Testament is from Habakkuk 2:5, where the word is used to describe the insatiable hunger of death itself. Sheol is understood as that morally neutral place to which everyone eventually goes, whether they have been good or evil. "The same fate comes to all, to the righteous and to the wicked, to the good and the evil" (Eccl. 9:2).

The injustice of an equal fate for all did trouble many of the writers. Job protests this injustice in an anguished cry: "It is all one; therefore I say, he destroys both the blameless and the wicked" (Job 9:22). The common belief was as expressed in Psalm 6:5, which asserts that "in death there is no remembrance of you; in Sheol who can give you praise?" Rabbi Stuart E. Rosenberg puts it succinctly: "In older Israel, as depicted in the Bible, death was the end of life and the dead went to a common abode of all who once lived: to the depths of the earth, called Sheol, or the netherworld."[1]

The foregoing thirty-one references to Sheol do not teach a future torture chamber for those who reject God's mercy. Death and judgment are underscored, but not "hell" as traditionally understood. We can be grateful for the work of recent translators who have made this more clear.

The Anger of God

A doctrine of hell, of course, is not simply based on the use of the word itself. God's anger or wrath is referred to about 375 times in the Old Testament. The Bible reveals a God of justice and love. It is precisely because of God's love for humans that his anger is kindled against us when we do sinful and disgusting things. God's anger, unlike much of ours, is never an irrational loss of self-control intending to punish or avenge. It is, in fact, one side of love. Because God cares, he cannot be indifferent to evil. An apathetic indifference does not point to a God of love.

Abraham Heschel has described God's wrath in the following terms:

> The anger of the Lord is instrumental, hypothetical, conditional, and subject to his will (Hos. 11:9). Let the people modify their line of conduct and anger will disappear (Jer. 19:7, 8). The call of anger is a call to cancel anger. . . . There is no divine anger for anger's sake. Its meaning is, as already said, instrumental: to bring about repentance; its purpose and consummation is its own disappearance.[2]

Anger and mercy are not seen as opposites in the Bible. Habakkuk prays that "in wrath may you remember mercy" (Hab. 3:2b). The psalmist pictures God as "slow to anger and abounding in steadfast love" (Ps. 145:8). It is correct to say, "God is love"; it is wrong to say, "God is wrath." Anger is an action of God, not a fundamental characteristic.

As Abraham Heschel has said, "Anger is an act, a situation, not an essential attribute."[3] Beyond anger lies the mystery of God's compassion. Isaiah exclaims that

In overflowing wrath for a moment I hid my face from you, but with everlasting love I will have compassion on you, says the Lord, your Redeemer. (Isa. 54:8)

Hosea records God's displeasure with Ephraim but adds, "I will not again destroy Ephraim; for I am God and no mortal, the Holy One in your midst, and I will not come in wrath" (Hos. 11:9).

Love is eternal. Anger will cease to be. No doctrine of eternal punishment can be deduced from the passages about God's wrath.

However, in Isaiah, Ezekiel, and Daniel we begin to find references to post mortem judgments that discriminate between the righteous and the evil. Isaiah hints at this in 26:19: "Your dead shall live, their corpses shall rise. O dwellers in the dust, awake and sing for joy!" Here is hope for the righteous after death.

Then in Daniel we read what sounds like the first actual reference to resurrection in the Hebrew Bible: "Many of those who sleep in the dust of the earth shall awake, some to everlasting life, and some to shame and everlasting contempt" (Dan. 12:2). While recognizing that this word for "everlasting" does not always mean "eternal," Robert Peterson sees this passage as teaching the contrasting "destinies of the righteous and the wicked."[4] And that it surely does.

However, this passage must be interpreted in its proper context as a vision, "not as a fully developed belief in resurrection."[5] John Goldingay, in his excellent commentary on Daniel, points out that the motif of the exposure of the wicked "has a this-world connotation."[6] "What is promised for the wicked is not eternal physical pain, but eternal shame."[7] This, in fact, was fulfilled for both the compromising Jews and Antiochus and his empire. Judgment is clearly taught. However, the ultimate doom of the wicked is vague.

Eternity Not Always Eternal

At this point it would be helpful for us to hear what linguistic scholars have found about the meaning of the Hebrew word *olam*, which we translate as "eternity." Depending upon its context it can mean "a long period, namely until the Messiah . . . will have completed the work of redemption on earth," or it may mean, "the whole period of the law," or "during this lifetime," or sometimes, "seventy-years."[8]

To Jeremiah God speaks of his anger burning "forever" (Jer. 17:4) and about making Jerusalem an "everlasting" disgrace (Jer. 25:9). But those are not the final words about the fate of Jerusalem. Jeremiah later states that "the fierce anger of the Lord will not turn back *until* he has executed and accomplished the intents of his mind" (Jer. 30:24). Isaiah similarly saw a judgment he calls "eternal" and then adds "*until* a spirit from on high is poured out on us*" (Isa. 32:14, 15, emph. added).

Jan Bonda says that

> Eternal punishment, however, does not forever continue, since that punishment itself is not his goal. When God's purpose has been achieved, there is no need for further punishment—for sin no longer exists. . . . Never is there any other purpose than that the unbeliever return to obedience to God. Nowhere in Scripture do we find a statement that tells us that God wants those who are punished to suffer without end—that is not the purpose for which God created humans.[9]

We must recognize then, that there is no clear teaching of a place of endless punishment in the Hebrew Bible, the Scriptures for first-century Christians. This would be one of the reasons why the apostles said very little about hell.

Mixed Messages

However, the Pharisees in Jesus' day did speak of a literal hell of ongoing punishment for the wicked. Stuart Rosenberg puts it like this:

> The Pharisees, however, came to believe in their own novel doctrine of individual retribution after death. . . . In short, God's justice would now be extended to the world to come, in anticipating the "end of time," each individual's merit or demerit would determine

whether he would be recreated, to emerge revivified after his time on earth.[10]

Those from the school of Hillel limited the judgment of the sinners to about a year with annihilation following.[11] The Apocryphal writings are not consistent—some articulate a destruction of the wicked (e.g. Wisdom of Solomon 4:18-19; 5:14, 15) and others an eternal existence of ongoing torment (e.g. I Enoch 27:1-3). There was no single view of hell among the Jews in Jesus' day and it is significant that there is almost no teaching of hell in Judaism today.

An example of current thinking is given in Rabbi Klenicki's dialogue with Richard Neuhaus. When asked by the Lutheran (now Catholic) pastor about his belief in an eternal destiny, Rabbi Leon Klenicki reflected the view of most of his Jewish contemporaries. He said,

> I think of death as a sort of eternal rest, a time of peace before the coming of the Messiah. I cannot imagine a hell and a paradise. For me, hell and paradise are here on earth. Auschwitz was a good representation of hell.[12]

How John Walvoord, Chancellor of Dallas Theological Seminary, can say that the Old Testament "clearly suggests that the sufferings of the wicked continue forever"[13] is surprising to me. The passages quoted above from the Old Testament are mostly eschatological in nature and these are always expressed in non-literal language. God's Spirit moved his servants to use poetic imagery, metaphors, surrealistic visions, and allegorical descriptions to picture the unseen future. Literalism can't work for hell any more than it could for heaven (unless you're expecting very large oysters to produce those "gates of pearl").

We must agree with Alan Bernstein that "there is no one statement that can describe the position of the Hebrew Bible on a given subject, certainly not on the question of divine punishment and justice." While most of its writers are resigned to a Sheol to which everyone ultimately goes, the latest writings include leanings toward a justice which may follow death. In defense of God's justice, "belief in punishment after death becomes necessary when no sign of restoration is visible in life."[14]

If the view of hell as perpetual punishment of the damned is not taught in the Old Testament, and was not part of the first-century apostolic preaching, how did it become a part of the Christian tradition as early as it did?

Tertullian in the third century spoke of everlasting torment for the unredeemed. In the *Didache* (a collection of early Christian writings used as a manual of instruction to train new converts put in final form sometime between 50 and 200 A.D.) we have the idea of annihilation as the fate of the unsaved.[15]

But after Augustine, in the latter part of the fourth century, the view of hell as he portrayed it was largely accepted by the church, namely that hell is a condition of endless torment for body and soul. Some have wondered if this understanding came as much from some of his own personal torments as it did from his theological explorations. God alone knows the answer to that. It is largely Augustine's carefully crafted doctrine of hell that has prevailed among Bible-believing Christians, who have largely insisted that Augustine's formulation is the teaching of the Bible.

So let us now consider what the Gospels tell us as they record for us the teachings of Jesus. For the Christian, Jesus' authority is always final.

4

Hell in the Gospels

*T*HE CONTENT OF APOSTOLIC PREACHING IS CRUCIAL to our understanding of how the first disciples interpreted the teachings of their Lord. With Jesus' validation of the authority of the Old Testament, this source also has to be considered for a better understanding of how they would use the word *hell.*

The Witness of Mark

Now we look directly into the Gospels to hear what Jesus taught about hell. Most scholars believe the Gospel according to Mark was the earliest written testimony to the deeds and sayings of Jesus. It is also believed that the apostle Peter may have provided material for Mark, so we will consider Mark's witness first.

Mark begins his Gospel with "the beginning of the good news of Jesus Christ, the Son of God" (Mark 1:1). His only reference to hell is not so much about hell as about the dangerous effects of certain offenses. Here Jesus is teaching the extreme seriousness of some sins that we might tend to excuse or minimize. To put "a stumbling block" before a child, to allow your hand, foot, or eye to cause you to stumble, can have disastrous results for others as well as for us. Misleading a little one, failing to discipline our gazing and acting may have seemed to Jesus' contemporaries and to us as minor offenses, but Jesus uses the strongest terms to challenge the popular view. Listen to his message:

If any of you put a stumbling block before one of these little ones who believe in me, it would be better for you if a great millstone were hung around your neck and you were thrown into the sea. If your hand causes you to stumble, cut it off; it is better for you to enter life maimed than to have two hands and to go to Hell, to the unquenchable fire. And if your foot causes you to stumble, cut it off; it is better for you to enter life lame than to have two feet and to be thrown into Hell. And if your eye causes you to stumble, tear it out; it is better for you to enter the kingdom of God with one eye than to have two eyes and to be thrown into hell, where the worm never dies, and the fire is never quenched. (Mark 9:42-48)

"A great millstone hung around the neck," "unquenchable fire," "hell, where their worm never dies,"—such are the colorful terms for God's judgment on those sins. The language is typical rabbinical hyperbole. The image of fire is a perfect metaphor for the fire of God's judgment. Jesus no more intended a literal description of hell than for his hearers to cut off their hands or legs or pluck out their eyes. Moreover, it is hardly consistent with all resurrection passages to imagine the saints rising with limbs or eyes missing!

Since we do not take literally the drowning with a great millstone around the neck, nor the mutilation of the body parts that offend, is it not inconsistent to take these references to hell as literal? Yet time after time does one read reference to this passage as proof that Jesus taught a literal hell!

Origin of Gehenna

It is probably appropriate here to examine the word translated as "hell." It is *Gehenna,* the name of the Valley of Hinnom, the ever-burning garbage dump southwest of Jerusalem. It had an evil history. Under the depraved leadership of King Ahaz, Israel was encouraged to worship the god Molech and burn little children there as an offering to this pagan god. King Josiah put a stop to that practice and labeled the area accursed. Thereafter Gehenna became a sort of public incinerator. Always the fire smoldered in it, a pall of thick smoke lay over it, and it bred a loathsome kind of worm that was hard to kill. Often the bodies of the worst criminals would be deposited here.

It is obvious that Jesus did not mean evil persons would literally burn in the Valley of Hinnom. So it must have been understood the way the Pharisees had—as symbolic of the state of unrepentant sinners. Fire could represent the burning of guilt, the sentence of holy justice, the purging away of evil, or a final destruction. Whatever the precise meaning intended, Jesus is making it clear that the judgment of God is unquestionable.

So the image of Gehenna was a powerful one clearly intended to shock hearers into paying attention. Jesus often used hyperbolic language like that, such as "Take the log out of your own eye" (Matt. 7:5). "Whoever does not hate his father and mother. . . . Whoever does not carry the cross and follow me cannot be my disciple" (Luke 14:26, 27). "It is easier for a camel to go through the eye of a needle than for someone who is rich to enter the kingdom of God" (Mark 10:25). "Let the dead bury their own dead" (Luke 9:60).

Certainly we do not take such statements literally. Language is not only used to convey information, it is used to stir emotion, provoke recognition, and challenge response. "Siren language" is what Helmut Thielicke has called the wording Jesus used about "hating" loved ones. We are as jarred by such terms as when we hear an emergency siren. We stop, look, and listen. "What does he mean by that?" we ask. That is exactly what Jesus intended.

Looking at John and Luke

When we read the Gospel of John we find no references to hell using either Hades or Gehenna. The reality of judgment is affirmed in words like, "perish," "condemned," and "shall not see life," but no use of the imagery of hell is used in what is likely the last gospel written. This harmonizes with the writings of Paul and all apostolic preaching as recorded in Acts.

Luke's Gospel, with a more Gentile audience in mind, makes only three references to hell—one uses the word Gehenna and two use Hades.

The Gehenna reference appears in the context of Pharisaic hostility and the impending persecution of Jesus' followers. So Jesus warns that they need not fear those who can, at worst, only kill their bodies. Our profoundest fear is to be given to the One who also lifts all fear from us. "Fear him who has authority to cast into hell . . . but even the hairs on your head are counted. Do not be afraid. . ." (Luke 12:5-7). Jesus' statement is not a threat but an encouragement. The worst an earthly foe can inflict is limited to this earth. God's justice determines the ultimate destiny of all, with effects going far beyond this earth (Matt. 10:28). "Fear the Lord" as the psalmists said. Then, Jesus assures us, all fear is gone.

The reference to Gehenna is a stark reminder of the seriousness of our lifetime orientation. Direction determines destiny. What we revere, honor, respect, and worship guides our lives. If God is not at the center of this life commitment, the image of Gehenna describes the tragic consequences. What these may be we cannot know in detail, but the paradoxical images of fire and darkness are ominous hints.

In Luke 10:15 Jesus warns those cities which have rejected his message that their fate could be more serious than that of Tyre and Sidon. To those in Capernaum, "will you be exalted to heaven? No, you will be brought down to Hades." Here is a prophetic word not unlike many in the Old Testament, where Sheol represents the judgment of death.

The parable of the rich man and Lazarus (Luke 16:19-31) is fascinating on several accounts but is clearly not intended to convey a literal description of hell. The word here is Hades, meaning "land of the dead." The message of God's requirement of mercy is central. The rich man's regret is too late. To reject God's Word—"Moses and the prophets"— means that even if someone rose from the dead, the rejecter would remain unmoved.

Unlike many of the parables of Jesus, this one does include strong allegorical overtones. The "great chasm has been fixed," warns us that there does come a time when it is "too late," when we "reap what we sow," when the consequences of earlier choices must inevitably be suffered. To ignore the poor, to withhold mercy from the needy, all the while selfishly faring sumptuously is clear evidence of rejecting the God of mercy. Such selfishness even blinds people to the reality of a risen Savior. The pictorial drama in Hades is an effective way to drive home the point.

To literalize the details is to rob the allegory of its power. Do we actually see Abraham from hell? Is conversation possible between hell and heaven? Are there microphones? Would a finger dipped in water cool the person burning in hell? Hardly. Does someone in hell desire the salvation of his brothers? Isn't that a caring expression? But love is not present in hell!

When you think about it, a literalistic interpretation of this passage sounds ridiculous. On the other hand, allowing the imagery to speak of God's values and wishes, and the consequences of showing mercy or failing to show mercy, is to be gripped by a powerful message indeed. The same would be true of the passage in Luke 13:27-30.

References to Hell in Matthew

Let us now consider the Gospel of Matthew. Here is where most of the references to hell are found, and they are all from the teachings of Jesus. It is said that "Jesus spoke more often of hell than he did of heaven."[1] This is grossly misleading. It is not even the case if the words heaven and hell are compared in a concordance. When we add "life," "eternal life," "my Father's house," "my joy," and "blessed are . . . ," we find a much greater emphasis on the positive possibilities than on the negatives.

Nevertheless, we now look carefully at how Matthew records our Lord's sayings about hell. Twice Jesus uses Hades, once to describe the judgment on Capernaum (Matt. 11:23) as noted earlier in Luke 10:15, and once in the charge to Peter, "On this rock I will build my church, and the gates of Hades will not prevail against it" (Matt. 16:18). Death has-n't a chance against the One who "is the resurrection and the life" (John 11:25), and the church is "his body."

Jesus and Gehenna in Matthew

It is our Lord's use of Gehenna that most conservative Christians build their doctrine of hell on. These include seven uses, beginning in the Sermon on the Mount with

> I say to you that if you are angry with a brother or sister, you will be liable to judgment, and if you insult a brother or sister, you will be liable to the council; and if you say, "You fool," you will be liable to the hell of fire. (Matt. 5:22)

Remembering that Jesus himself used the term "fool" for certain Pharisees (Matt. 23:17), we are well advised against using a literalistic interpretation here.

What Jesus is teaching here is the evil of undisciplined anger. He offers what appear to be three levels of anger and corresponding gradations of punishment. The first expression of anger refers to a brooding, inveterate, undying anger against another. Such a person should be brought before the village elders. All lingering selfish anger needs to be removed from the hearts of God's children.

The second form of anger is expressed by the insults. The word is *Raca*, an expression of arrogant contempt. The person who looks down on another and hurls contempt at him ought to be brought before the supreme court of the Jews, the Sanhedrin. The third level of anger is expressed by calling someone a "fool"—implying in this case, a moral fool, branding someone a "godless loose-liver." Such a one is liable to "hell fire."

How calling someone a "fool" deserves "hell," while calling someone "Raca" (idiot) only calls for the Sanhedrin, is baffling if taken at face value. But as most commentators point out, none of those three punishments are to be taken literally. Anger in Israel then, as in America today, does not bring you into court unless you express it in some hurtful manner toward someone else. Jesus warns us that while murder is clearly a reprehensible act deserving of judgment, so is anger in all its varied forms of insults and contemptuous attitudes.

Since the Pharisees did believe in a literal hell, this reference would drive home the seriousness of the offense. But a trip to a literal hell is not being taught here any more than calling someone Raca earned them an actual appointment with the Sanhedrin council. As William Barclay puts it,

> As we have said, all these gradations of punishment are not to be taken literally. What Jesus is saying here is this: In the old days men condemned murder; and truly murder is forever wrong. But I tell you that not only are a man's outward actions under judgment; his inmost thoughts are also under the scrutiny and the judgment of God. Long-lasting anger is bad; contemptuous speaking is worse, and the careless or the malicious talk which destroys a man's good name is the worst of all. The man who is the slave of anger, the man who speaks in the accent of contempt, the man who destroys another's good name, may never have committed a murder in action, but he is a murderer at heart.[2]

I'm not sure I can fully agree with Barclay that calling someone a fool is worse than calling him Raca. Nevertheless the point to be made is that Jesus' teaching here is ethical, not predictive. Robert Guelich hits the nail on the head when he hears Jesus deliberately using

> irony to get at the underlying relationships between people. Whereas the Law had prohibited murder arising from broken relationships. . . . Jesus ultimately demands a relationship between individuals in which there is no alienation.[3]

If calling someone a fool merits hell, what do we say about Jesus' use of that word for the rich farmer (Luke 12:20) or for the Pharisees (Luke 11:40)?

In Matthew 5:29, 30 we have the same idea as we considered in Mark 9:42-48. Adultery was forbidden as the seventh commandment, but Jesus again goes to the heart of the problem and condemns lust. Jesus recognizes that it is first of all the inclination of the mind and heart, then the roving eyes and groping hands that lead to adulterous behavior. He prescribes radical self-discipline—"tear out your eye," "cut off your hand." These are obviously not intended to be taken literally, any more than envisioning whole bodies in hell or maimed ones in heaven. This teaching is not so much about final destiny as it is about curbing lustful desires before they create a hellish harvest. The same emphasis is present again in Matthew 18:9.

The sentence for hypocrisy

Our Lord's disappointment in the Pharisees is evident in his frequent condemnation of their hypocrisy. In Matthew 23:15 he calls them children "of hell." In verse 33 he makes his harshest judgment: "You snakes, you brood of vipers! How can you escape being sentenced to hell?" "Snakes," "vipers," and "hell" constitute dramatic language underscoring the seriousness of God's judgment. The chapter is filled with our Lord's indictment of the religious leadership of his day. Six times Jesus begins his denunciations with "Woe to you, scribes and Pharisees, hypocrites" and once "Woe to you, blind guides."

 Apparently God's greatest displeasure is not vented against "tax-collectors and prostitutes." It is against persons in my position of religious leadership. Jesus said of these, "They do not practice what they teach" (Matt. 23:3). I must ask, "What will God say to me on that day?"

Those who represent God must not misrepresent him. To burden folks and not offer the slightest help is a denial of the God of mercy (v. 4). To keep people from entering the kingdom of heaven by burdening them with impossible requirements (v. 13) is a denial of the God who is not willing that any should perish. To concentrate on minor issues and neglect the weightier matters (v. 23) is a denial of God's perspective. To focus on externals and ignore the motives of the heart (vv. 25-28) is to deny the priorities of God. Such hypocrisy is as poisonous as a brood of vipers.

God's judgment—"the sentence to hell"—is a real possibility. "How can you escape?" is the question. The implied
answer is that there is no escape from the judgment of such
hypocrisy, such distorting of the image of God—except by
repentance and surrender to the God of mercy and justice.
The language could not be more powerful in expressing
God's displeasure with hypocrisy. Judgment is real. The
word hell does appropriately describe this judgment.

In Summary

It seems to come down to this. The thirty-one references
to hell in the Old Testament are all translations of the word
Sheol, meaning the grave or region of the dead. In the King
James Version of the New Testament, of the twenty-three
times the word hell appears, ten are in reference to Hades,
which is similar in meaning to Sheol. There is one use of Tartaros in Peter that refers to a judgment of angels and the thir-
teen other uses are from the word *Gehenna*, the garbage dump
outside of Jerusalem. These references include the element
of judgment, but the word itself is nearly always metaphoric
in how it is used. In other words, there is no clear teaching
of a literal hell in which sinners are tortured endlessly.

However, There Is More

"Hold it," I hear someone saying. "Belief in an eternal
hell is not solely based on the use of the word hell itself."
That is correct. We read of "eternal fire" in Matthew 18:8,
25:41 and "eternal punishment" in Matthew 25:46. What can
these mean other than the plain teaching of an "eternal" hell?

We need to remember how the word *eternal* was used in
the Hebrew Bible. We noted in the last chapter that eternal
did not necessarily mean without end. It always meant that
period of time until God's "purpose was accomplished."[4]
Isaiah gives a classic example:

> The palace will be forsaken, the populous city deserted,
> the hill and the watchtower will become dens *forever* . . .
> until the Spirit is poured upon us from on high. (Isa.
> 32:14, 15, emph. added)

Jesus used the Hebrew Bible and understood its meaning, so there was no need for him to qualify his use of the word translated "forever" or "eternal." Karl Barth describes eternal justice in these words: "It judges men absolutely. It utterly abandons them. It burns them right down to *faith*."[5] Then God's plan is fulfilled. Nowhere do we read that God wants sinners to suffer without end.

Eternal Life Is Divine Life

Some will argue that to infer that hell is not eternal jeopardizes belief in eternal life. Such an argument is seriously flawed. Any adjective must be understood in relation to the noun it modifies. Eternal life has to do with life with God, life without sin or death, life in the "Father's house." When the adjective *eternal* is used with *judgment,* it is referring to that ominous span of time required to achieve the holy will of God. It could not mean an endless period of time, since such would be both pointless and contradict God's purpose for his created family.

That purpose is more clearly revealed in the parables of the lost and found as recorded in Luke 15. God was not satisfied with ninety-nine safe if one was lost. Nine silver coins were not satisfactory if there were to be ten. The father's joy was not complete with one righteous son if the other was lost. Jesus is telling us that God's purposes are fulfilled when the lost are found and the whole family is together at last.

Does not this fit with the kingdom ethic of overcoming evil with good? Jesus calls us "to be perfect" as our "heavenly Father is perfect" (Matt. 5:48). The context makes clear that we are to act and react with the same kind of love the Father extends to us. "If anyone strikes you on the right cheek, turn the other also" (v. 39). "Love your enemies and pray for those who persecute you so that you may be children of your Father in heaven" (vv. 44,45). When Peter asks how often he is to forgive Jesus replies, "not seven times, but seventy-seven (or seventy times seven) times" (Matt. 18:22).

If this is the ethic required of us, how can we imagine that our Lord would do less?

5

Judgment in the Epistles

*J*ESUS IS OUR POINT OF REFERENCE FOR UNDERSTANDING the Hebrew Bible. His interpretation was what the apostles received
and passed on. Our Christian faith is built on their witness
to the life, death, resurrection, and teachings of our Lord
Jesus Christ. We must believe that what Jesus emphasized,
they would in turn also stress.

No Threats of Hell

In writing to the churches, the apostles address individual situations to which they apply the precepts and principles of the grace and goodness of God as revealed in Jesus
Christ. Salvation is the "gift" of God (Eph. 2:8), and the character and conduct of the Christian is the "work" of grateful
response (Phil. 2:12). The missionary assignment is described
as a "ministry of reconciliation" making "us ambassadors
for Christ" (2 Cor. 5:20).

It is noteworthy to observe that nowhere is the church
enjoined to rescue people from hell. The motive in their evangelism is to proclaim Good News precisely because it is such *LOST THAT GOAL*
"good news"! To be forgiven. To be welcomed by the Creator
as Savior. To find direction for life and what follows through
allegiance to Jesus Christ as Lord. To become fully free and
alive in the family where love predominates and God is now
called "Father." These are the blessings that prompt the sharing of the gospel. The threat of hell seems to play little part.

As a matter of fact, it must be noted that hell as a translation of Hades or Gehenna does *not* appear in *any* of the epistles. Paul never uses the word Gehenna, and his only use of the word Hades is in celebration of its defeat (1 Cor. 5:54, 55). The only use of hell is in 2 Peter 2:4 where it translates the word *tartaros*, referring to a temporary destination of fallen angels, "kept until the judgment."

Since Jesus did use the words for hell, how do we explain their absence in the writings of his apostles? Robert A. Peterson, who believes the apostles did teach an "eternal hell," concedes that they tend to be less pointed in their descriptions of hell than Jesus was. Quoting from W. G. T. Shedd, he sees this as an expression of humility in their reluctance to "delineate the nature and consequences of the sentence."[1]

There may be a better answer. The apostles may have recognized better than we do the true meaning of the words Jesus used for hell and so, when they referred to judgment, they used terms their recipients, mostly Gentiles, could better understand. They would not want their Gentile converts to associate terms for hell with their pagan ideas. More on those ideas in the next chapter.

After analyzing the Pauline letters, Alan Bernstein notes what he calls a tension between "destruction, punishment, and reconciliation"[2] as the fate of the wicked. Was Paul confused? Could he not decide? We might suggest one of those options if we did not believe that God's Spirit had something to do with what he wrote. I believe therefore that we need to hear the message in each of these themes.

It is enlightening to note in Crockett's *Four Views on Hell* how the different authors choose their supporting biblical texts. Walvoord picks out those verses that suggest eternal punishment. Pinnock quotes those verses that teach the annihilation of the wicked. When we read Jan Bonda's *The One Purpose of God* we see the selection of those passages which point to an ultimate restoration of all people.

They are all conscientiously attempting to understand the Bible. Maybe they each are sharing important truths. Certainly "the wages of sin is death" (Rom. 6: 23) or "destruction" (Thess. 5:3) because every good we can know or experience is destroyed when corrupted by sin. Certainly we all deserve the punishment of a just and holy God when we violate the ways of truth and love. "For those who are self seeking and who obey not the truth but wickedness, there will be a wrath and fury. There will be anguish and distress . . ." (Rom. 2: 8, 9). Yet in the same letter Paul also writes, "God has imprisoned all in disobedience so that he may be merciful to all" (Rom. 11:32) and at last "every knee shall bow to me, and every tongue shall give praise to God" (Rom. 14:11). An ultimate restoration or reconciliation is also taught.

Now let us look at some of the passages that declare the judgment of God.

The Wrath of God

The letters of the apostles make clear the seriousness of violating the will of God. Rebellion against God and God's ways results in terrible consequences for the sinner in both this life and more justly in the life to come. One phrase often used is the "wrath of God."

> For the wrath of God is revealed from heaven against all ungodliness and wickedness of those who . . . suppress the truth. (Rom. 1:18)

> . . . the day of wrath, when God's righteous judgment will be revealed. (Rom. 2:5)

> . . . for those who are self-seeking and who obey not the truth but wickedness, there will be wrath and fury. (Rom. 2:8)

> The wrath of God comes on those who are disobedient. (Eph. 5:6)

> Jesus, who rescues us from the wrath that is coming. (1 Thess. 1:10)

For those who opposed Paul and the spreading of the gospel, the apostle says that God's wrath has already overtaken them, (1 Thess. 2:16) referring to their judgment by God either by their death or by their incapacity to hinder the work of spreading the gospel any longer. What is taught in the letters to the churches is the reality of corresponding consequences following our actions.

> For he will repay according to each one's deeds. (Rom. 1:6)

> For all of us must appear before the judgment seat of Christ, so that each may receive recompense for what he has done in the body, whether good or evil. (2 Cor. 5:10)

> Do not be deceived; God is not mocked, for you reap whatever you sow. If you sow to your own flesh, you will reap corruption from the flesh; but if you sow to the Spirit, you will reap eternal life from the Spirit. (Gal. 6:7, 8)

While consequences may follow our actions in this life, the perfect settlement occurs on the "Day of Judgment" (Rom. 1:5; 2:16;1 Cor. 3:13; 2 Pet. 3:10).

Judgment Day Surprise

So it is quite clear that judgment is recognized. But does this mean endless suffering for sinners? Paul was a Pharisee, and we know Pharisees did hold to a literal hell using the word Gehenna. Yet, as noted earlier, Paul nowhere uses Gehenna.

What does he then mean by God's judgment? Paul affirms a God of justice and righteousness. He also affirms human accountability. How God will execute justice in terms of manner, method, or duration, he leaves with the wisdom of God. But that a day of judgment lies ahead for the whole world is not in doubt (Acts 17:31).

What must also be noted, however, is that Paul is as eager to share an optimistic view of the ultimate future. His use of "all" is significant. At this point believers in divine inspiration need to be consistent. The context of these verses does not preclude taking "all" quite literally. To argue that these verses should only refer to the "elect-saved" is to impose an interpretation from an *a priori* decision to rule out the possibility of an ultimate salvation for all.

So let us leave that judgment behind us and hear what the apostle is, in fact, saying:

> Therefore, just as one man's trespass led to condemnation for *all*, so one man's act of righteousness leads to justification and life for *all*. (Rom. 5:18, emph added here and below)

> For God has imprisoned *all* in disobedience so that he may be merciful to *all*. (Rom. 11:32)

> . . . from him and through him and to him are all things. To him be the glory forever. Amen. (Rom. 11:36)

> For it is written, "As I live, says the Lord, *every* knee shall bow to me, and *every* tongue shall give praise to God." (Rom. 14:11)

> As *all* die in Adam, so *all* will be made alive in Christ. (1 Cor. 15:22)

Ultimately "God will be *all in all*" (1 Cor. 15:28). What does this say about hell? Are we not being given the message that hell is not eternal? To the Ephesians Paul states God's plan for the fullness of time to gather up "*all* things in him" (Eph. 1:10, emph. added). The early hymn of the church quoted to the Philippians concludes with the promise that

> at the name of Jesus *every* knee should bend, in heaven and on earth and under the earth, and *every* tongue should confess that Jesus Christ is Lord, to the glory of God the Father. (Phil. 2:10-11)

And to the Colossians Paul emphasizes that "God was pleased to reconcile to himself *all* things, whether on earth or in heaven, by making peace through the blood of his cross"(Col. 2:21).

All Judged So All May Be Saved?

Is this universalism? If that means we can all live as we please and it will all turn out fine in the end, I reject the term. If it means there is no belief in hell, I emphatically reject the label. My attempt is to understand what Paul was saying by all of those inclusive references to a day of final reconciliation. They appear to point to a day of universal restoration. What Paul means is what I am struggling to affirm.

I hesitate to set forth any view that fails to harmonize with the great Christian theologians past or present who no doubt may have given more time and thought to this subject than I have. But a statement by John Stott has been helpful. He writes, "The hallmark of an authentic evangelicalism is not the uncritical repetition of old traditions, but the willingness to submit every tradition, however ancient, to fresh scrutiny and if necessary reform."[3]

Obviously I feel strongly that the ancient doctrine of an eternal hell needs reform. What I am opting for is a recognition of *both* the judgment passages and the universal salvation passages. Most Christians recognize that both divine election and human free will are taught in Scripture. Both faith and works are stressed. Exactly how these truths always come together we may not understand, but we affirm both.

A simplistic approach is to opt for "either-or." A wiser approach surely will recognize the power in paradox. The apparent contradiction is only what we perceive now. Some day, the curtains will part and, as the old gospel song has it, "We'll understand it better bye and bye."

For now let us affirm what the Bible teaches. There is salvation for all in Christ. There is a day of judgment and separation. Some are welcomed. Some are rejected (Matt. 25:32-46). Judgment, the wrath of God, falls on those who have rebelled against God's ways. Then—how long is unknown—ultimately the victory is won for all and "every knee bows" and "every tongue praises God" (Rom. 14:11).

Since "eternal" in the Hebrew Bible does not mean "endless days"[4] this surely must have been the understanding of Jesus and his disciples. In other words, hell is that state in which God's judgment is executed *until* repentance is made and then redemption is given. God is the Lord of both the living and the dead, so we dare not limit God's grace to the brief experience of our few days on earth. The Catholic doctrine of Purgatory attempts to work with this reality.

As stated earlier, I cannot harmonize the doctrine of election with free will, but both are taught and each conveys an important truth that must not be lost. Judgment is taught. So is an ultimate redemption of the whole universe. I will affirm both. I cannot dilute the seriousness of judgment. God is holy! But I look forward to the final hour when all things are new again and, as my friend Dr. Robert Johnston likes to say, "God's YES is always bigger than his NO!" Amen.

6

Origins of Belief in Hell

"SOME CONCEPTIONS OF HEAVEN AND HELL are found universally among the religions of the world."[1] The belief that life in some form continues after death seems to be held by most people (outside of the comparatively small atheist circle). Together with this sense of ongoing life, there is felt the need for some vision of heaven or hell to set things right ultimately, since pure justice for all is nonexistent on this planet. Future reward or punishment seemed necessary to give meaning to life in the present.

The details of these ultimate destinations vary greatly, but generally they are described in terms of a spiritual direction. There is a "Great Above," a region of bliss, and there is a "Great Below," a region of pain. This teaching of a heaven and a hell has also been a part of Christian doctrine from the beginning.

History of Hell

How heaven and hell are described, together with our affirmations about who goes where, have, however not always harmonized with the teachings of our Lord. Everything we proclaim must be consistent with the manner and message of Jesus Christ if it is to be recognized as a distinctly Christian understanding. It may be that what we have assumed was a part of our Lord's teachings may not, on closer examination, be the case.

The images of hell go back over 4000 years, as Alice Turner notes in her *History of Hell*. The gods of Mesopotamia consigned evildoers to a torturous nether region filled with demons and fire. What is fascinating to note, however, is that in some of these ancient accounts certain gods or goddesses would actually descend into hell to rescue one or more victims of the evil gods.

Egypt also had its descriptions of hell. The souls who were hell-doomed were those whose good works did not measure up when weighed against a feather from the headdress of Maat, the goddess of truth. Then the god Osiris, the judge of all, would pronounce sentence. Hindus have many hells (several million) and "Buddhists count from eight hells to several thousand."[2] In most cases these are not eternal consignments, but more of a purgation experience along the route of numerous reincarnations.

Although Zoroastrian written material comes many years after Christianity, some stories precede the birth of Christ and include the need for every person to appear before the wise Lord Ohrmazd. Should they fail to measure up by a strict mathematical code—"even three small acts of wrongdoing"—they will be consigned to hell ruled by the evil spirit Ahriman. In Zoroastrianism there is also the hope of a final "harrowing" of hell by a savior figure called Soshyans, then hell itself will be destroyed. This understanding may have come after the birth of Christianity and could have been influenced by it.

The Greco-Roman world in which Christianity was born was filled with gods and goddesses, but here the separation of good and evil was not clearly made. Their deities were a mix of both virtues and vices. Plato and some of the poet-philosophers tried to clarify a difference between good and evil and so designated their versions of heaven and hell. The poet Hesiod speaks of the birth of Tartaros—the word used for hell by the apostle Peter (2 Pet. 2:4)—as resulting from a battle of the gods where the defeated were thrown into a "place far below the earth" surrounded by a bronze wall and guarded by the "Hound of Hell."

How much influence these views of hell may have had on the church is not clear. Some effect is no doubt inevitable. Culture regularly plays its part in flavoring or poisoning the Christian witness. We need only to remember the church's centuries-old acquiescence to its cultures in support of slavery, its justifications of violence, male domination of women, and other un-Christ-like behavior patterns, to realize that what we have often touted as "pure doctrine" has not always been so pure.

Influence of Judaism

Of stronger influence in early Christianity, however, would have been the teachings and writings of Judaism at the time. When we read the Apocrypha we begin to understand why the Pharisees believed in a literal hell (although the Sadducees and some other sects did not). In 2 Esdras 7:36 (NEB here and below) we read of the destiny of all people, "Then the place of torment shall appear, and over against it the place of rest; the furnace of Hell shall be displayed, and on the opposite side the paradise of delight."

The hardness of heart evident among many who were teaching about eternal punishment has a precedent in what Esdras supposedly heard God say. "I shall have joy in the few who are saved . . . but I shall not grieve for the many who are lost" (2 Esdras 7:60).

This hint may have led to the grosser expression given by Augustine, where he relates that believers in heaven, far from being disturbed by the suffering of the wicked, will actually receive a sense of satisfaction in viewing their hellish torments. He wrote, "the unjust will burn to some extent so that all the just in the Lord may see the joys that they receive and in those may look upon the punishments which they have evaded."[3] Thomas Aquinas also shared that view. William Crockett comments that "to say that the blessed will delight in the torture of the damned is hard to imagine, especially if the damned include loved ones."[4]

Such a perspective does not sound like it could come from the One who wept over Jerusalem and offered forgiveness to all his enemies from the cross. I am not suggesting that Augustine or Aquinas were not good Christians and great theologians, but like all of us, they had their blind spots, and here we may see one of them.

Again from 2 Esdras 7:79, 80 the message is clear: "As for those who have rejected the ways of the Most High . . . their spirits enter no settled abode, but roam thenceforth in torment, grief, and sorrow." In 9:13 those who failed to acknowledge God in their lifetime will "learn the truth through torments after death." In the Wisdom of Solomon both the destruction of the wicked (4:18, 19) as well as their lasting torment (17:3-21) seem to be taught. The same idea is also expressed in the Pseudepigrapha (1 Enoch 27:1-3).

Some writers became excessive in their lurid descriptions of hell as a gruesome torture chamber. As Crockett quotes Lieberman,

> Jewish literature is often more graphic than the frightful descriptions of hell found in the Christian apocalypses. The rabbis speak of licentious men hanging by their genitals, women who publicly suckle children hanging by their breasts, and those who talked during synagogue prayers having their mouths filled with hot coals.[5]

The Bible, however, is more interested in other subjects. Judgment is affirmed. What happens to those who reject God's grace is deadly serious. It is understandable that refusal to accept a gift means one is without it. Judgment before an all-holy and all-loving Creator is declared. But the details of what this judgment entails are not always clear, and some even sound self-contradictory, such as "lake of fire" or "outer darkness."

Hell Is Enlarged

By the third century, however, this judgment of the unrighteous took on frightening terms. Tertullian was one of the church fathers who in 200-212 did not hesitate to elucidate on the pains and agonies of the damned.

Then the eloquent and brilliant theologian of the late fourth and early fifth century, Augustine, Archbishop of Hippo, gave substance to what would be the orthodox position of both Catholic and Reformed churchmen. In his articulation he made hell a literal abode of unrepentant sinners. It is interesting to note that in his earlier years he had difficulty with Old Testament stories until Bishop Ambrose of Milan helped him to understand that some of these accounts could be treated as allegories.[6] One wonders why the same approach did not occur to him for understanding some of the "hell passages," especially those in the obviously apocalyptic and allegorical book of Revelation.

From the time of Augustine through the period of the Reformers, Luther and Calvin, the eternal damnation of the wicked has been accepted as a doctrine of Christian orthodoxy. The doctrine of hell became most popular between 400 and 1400 AD. It was refined, painted, preached, and luridly envisioned by authors and playwriters whose depictions might be called a form of "santified pornography." The most sensational portrayal of hell was made by Dante in his *Inferno*, circulated around 1314. His nine descending catagories of punishment for nine types of sins intrigued artists for centuries. In one sense, however, he helped kill belief in a literal hell by making it fictional and allegorical.

But the church was not ready to deliteralize hell. In the Catholic tradition, "If anyone dies unrepentant in the state of mortal sin, he will undoubtedly be tormented forever in the fires of an everlasting Hell" (Pope Innocent IV, 1224). "If anyone says that the punishments of the damned in Hell will not last forever, let him be anathema" (Vatican 1, 1870). More recently, Pope John Paul II stated that "hell is a spiritual state, not a physical place. It is the state of those who freely and definitively separate themselves from God."[7]

In the Reformed tradition, the Westminster Confession states that the "non-elect shall be cast into eternal torments and be punished with everlasting destruction" (33.2). In a Baptist creedal statement, "The unrighteous will be consigned to Hell, the place of everlasting punishment."[8]

On July 8, 1741 Jonathan Edwards, a New England minister, preached his memorable message on "Sinners in the
Hands of An Angry God." In it he said,

> The God that holds you over a pit of Hell, much as one
> holds a spider . . . over the fire, abhors you and is dread-
> fully provoked. His wrath toward you burns like fire:
> He looks upon you as worthy of nothing else but to be
> cast into the fire; He is of purer eyes than to bear to have
> you in His sight; you are ten thousand time more abom-
> inable in His eyes than the most hateful venomous ser-
> pent is in ours.[9]

I wonder: Did Edwards ever considered if Jesus would
say that? Edward's hell is a spiritual and material furnace of
fire where its victims are exquisitely tortured in their minds
and in their bodies eternally. This is hardly consistent with
the grace and mercy we find in Jesus, or even with his angri-
est outbursts of overturning "the tables of the money chang-
ers and the seats of those who sold doves" (Mark 11:15).

Would the common people have heard Jesus gladly—as
Mark 12:37 puts it, "The large crowd was listening to him
with delight"—if he had been sounding like Edwards? If one
looks again at the "hell passages," most are reserved for religious leaders guilty of hypocrisy! (Matt. 23:13-36). The aver-
age person, including tax collectors and the morally defi-
cient, enjoyed Jesus' company and his teachings. That would
not be true for a judgmental "condemner-to-hell" person.

The Accommodation Factor

The belief in a literal hell of lasting duration was an accommodation to prevailing beliefs. At first, while the church
was young and opposed by the world, the world it would
seek to evangelize, there was little preaching of hell (none in
Acts). Believers were persecuted, given "hellish" treatment,
but rarely called their enemies hell-bound. Origen, a brilliant
Christian teacher in Caesarea during the early 200s, even believed everyone would be saved eventually.

But after Constantine and the rise of the state-sanctioned
church, the cruelest edges of the doctrine of hell were sharp-

ened. From 315 A.D. on the church was controlled and supported by the state. A cruel hell might be considered an effective tool in maintaining political order. The threat of such
a hell was in fact often so used throughout the Middle Ages.

It is also evident that, except for the devout few, understanding of God's grace was largely lost. Few could read.
Few even knew the stories of Jesus except as they were told,
often by those lacking an experience of personal salvation.
Hell could even be made more believable by the "hell" of the
Inquisition the church unleashed on dissenters. If God's
church does that on earth, why believe God will act differently in the next world? Does the church not represent God?

Accommodation to the prevailing culture is something
to which we all are susceptible. Martin Luther stands on the
Word of God and courageously challenges papal infallibility
and the corrupt practice of selling indulgences (to lessen
years in purgatory). Then he reflects the culture's prejudice
in ugly assertions of anti-Semitism.

John Calvin, brilliant theologian and devoted believer,
at age twenty-three writes the classic "Institutes of the Christian Religion." Then he consents to the burning of Cervetes,
whose theology was considered heretical.

It was a cruel age, reflecting ignorance of the gospel of
God's love even among some who were scholars and teachers of the Bible. Reformers caught insights from Scripture but
yielded to the ways of their world in handling opposing
views. The treatment of Anabaptists in the Netherlands and
in Switzerland shows a total disregard for the teachings of
Christ's love and mercy. Our Lord challenged his followers
to love and pray for their enemies and these were not even
enemies; they were brothers and sisters! When Menno Si-
mons reminded the church of Jesus' word of blessing on
peacemakers and the Lord's call to refrain from violence and
"turn the other cheek," he and his followers were assaulted
by both Protestants and Catholics.

Is it that in an era of cruelty, where the love of God has
been largely unrecognized or forgotten, the teaching of a
cruel hell can survive and flourish? For whatever reasons,

the doctrine of hell became entrenched in church tradition, and as we know, traditions are hard to change. They become an integral part of our culture, which the church is often inclined to support in the interests of social stability.

Influence of Prevailing Culture

Was this not the case in America, where for years the church sanctioned and supported the institution of slavery? Bible-believing preachers found in Scripture all the support they needed. There are, in fact, as many verses that can be used to support slavery as verses on hell. One need only read Exodus 21:2-6, 20, 21; Leviticus 25:44-46; and, in the New Testament, Ephesians 6:5; Colossians 3:22, 4:1; and 1 Peter 2:18-21. No explicit condemnation of slavery can be cited from the Bible. So those who took the Scriptures literally found abundant support for their justification of slavery.

In 1856 a Baptist minister, Thorton Stringfellow, said this: "Jesus Christ recognized this institution as one that is lawful among men and regulated its relative duties."[10] When in 1845 the Baptist General Convention, through its executive board, issued a statement no longer approving slavery, a group withdrew to form what is now the largest Protestant denomination in the United States, the Southern Baptist Convention. Finally in 1995 an official apology was offered, but racism still lingers among us.

Did all Christians support slavery before 1840? Thankfully, no. Among those who rejected it as evil were those who let Jesus Christ be their guide to understanding what God intended by those numerous references to slavery. They saw in them a description of how society was, not how it ought to be. They saw the spirit of Jesus more accurately reflected in Paul's letter to Philemon where he implores his friend to receive the run-away slave, Onesimus, back "no longer as a slave, but more than a slave, a beloved brother" (Phil. 1:16).

That echoed the heart of God as long before described in these lines from Isaiah 58:6: "Is this not the fast that I choose: to loose the bonds of injustice, to undo the thongs of the yoke, to let the oppressed go free, and to break every yoke." This passage was quoted in a Quaker document opposing slavery in 1760.[11] It seems a main reason so many Christians condoned slavery at that time was as an accommodation to their culture, supported by proof-texting from the Bible.

In some respects the same situation prevails today among many evangelicals with regard to belief in a literal torturous hell. It started early, before biblical days, with Mesopotamian and Egyptian mythology. Then came the Greco-Roman versions and the teachings in the Apocrypha. The Pharisees affirmed hell as did some writers of the Pseudopigrapha. Although not taught in the Old Testament or proclaimed by the apostles of Christ, the references in the New Testament to divine judgment were soon colored by the cultural imagery. By the time the church was institutionalized, the doctrine of eternal punishment for nonbelievers was intact. As with the justification of slavery, there were verses enough to justify a belief in hell.

Accommodation to cultural values and beliefs is all too easy. Some televangelists justify their worldly extravagance by labeling it a reward-blessing from God. Preaching against homosexuality is more popular than condemning greed and luxury. The fact that Jesus spoke far more of the dangers of wealth than about sexual sins is ignored by such "Bible-believers." We are all tempted to go with the flow, to become political and say what our hearers most enjoy hearing. After all, don't we want their donations?

Accepting the Challenge

In the world of evangelical scholarship there are accepted doctrines one can only challenge at risk of being branded heretical. Some who supported the emancipation of slaves or equal rights of women received such labels. Thankfully there are today a number of godly, careful, Bible-believing scholars who are challenging the traditional understanding of hell. Their writings not only examine the grammatical-historical meaning of a text, but, looking at the larger context, seek to discover how what is said fits with the supreme revelation of God's truth in Christ.

This is a needed corrective to the numerous books defending the traditional view of hell. In these we read one proof text after another but little about the moral implications when considered beside the character of Christ.

Clark Pinnock is, I believe, right when he says that "any doctrine of hell needs to pass the moral test."[12] Slavery could not pass. Nor does a God who tortures people endlessly. Yet this view is inscribed in the creedal statements of most Christian denominations and changing these, even if the effort is toward a more Christ-like position, is often tantamount to heresy. Remember the words of John Stott, quoted earlier: "The hallmark of an authentic evangelicalism is not the uncritical repetition of old traditions but the willingness to submit every tradition, however ancient, to fresh scrutiny and, if necessary, reform."[13]

I believe one tradition in need of reform is a literalistic reading of Scripture, which is often linked to teaching an eternal hell for sinners. So in such books as *The Population of Heaven*, by Ramask P. Richard, many prooftexts are selected to support the traditional view of hell. Yet when examined in context, it can be shown that the image of hell offered in such texts may be interpreted as a metaphor, an allegorical image, or a hyperbolic term used to emphasize the seriousness of Christ's teaching.

Taking such references literalistically, however, allows Richard to conclude that "Those who have heard and rejected the gospel are doubly at eternal fault. Those who have not heard nor rejected the gospel are singularly at eternal fault (therefore hell-bound)."[14] Focusing on texts about hell as if they are photographic descriptions makes this seem the inevitable conclusion, but the question is whether literalism faithfully conveys the true meaning of such texts.

In the next chapter I want to challenge this view of Scripture. I do not think it is a doctrine held by Jesus or the apostles. A "higher" view of Scripture would call us to receive its message as the authors intended and as harmonized with the revelation of God in Christ.

The Problem of a Literalistic Approach

*I*N AN ARTICLE IN *CHRISTIANITY TODAY,* Timothy George stated, "The authority of the gospel is established by the authority of the Bible."[1] Without question our celebration of God's love in redemption includes our gratitude to God for providing for us a trustworthy written source of knowledge about it.

No doubt this was part of the motivation of the framers of the Lousanne Covenant of 1974, in which Article 2 states the trustworthiness of the Bible as "without error in all that it affirms." This was reaffirmed in the "Chicago Statement on Biblical Inerrancy in 1978," and at a second conference in 1982 sixteen papers were presented addressing various hermeneutic principles.

I received copies of many of the papers presented at this conference. Some were fine scholarly contributions. But the voluminous attempts by others, often committed to defending "inerrant" Scripture, to explain "apparent inconsistencies" or "difficult passages" seemed counter-productive. For some to suggest that these difficulties may not have existed in the original manuscripts seemed an inadequate explanation, since we do have some pretty old documents. On the positive side, however, emphasis was given to the importance of principles of interpretation, which include learning the author's intent as well as recognizing the grammatical, cultural, and historical context of a passage.

Biblical Authority

I often wonder why Bible-believing Christians don't simply take the Bible's own statement about its inspiration and authority. Paul wasted no time in confusing Timothy with a universal negative—such as making the unprovable claim of "no errors." Rather, he affirmed the positive in a way that declares both the authority and purpose of divine inspiration. Paul reminded Timothy that "the sacred writings are able to instruct you for salvation through faith in Christ Jesus." Then he added, "All Scripture is inspired by God and is useful for teaching, for reproof, for correction, for training in righteousness, so that everyone may be proficient, equipped for every good work" (2 Tim. 3:15-17).

Useful is the inspired word. Useful can be proved in every person who has been blessed and led by the word of God. The intent was to bring us to salvation and make us all proficient and equipped for good works. The emphasis is clearly on character and conduct development. The focus here is *not* on scriptural flawlessness.

Inerrancy defenders will remind us of Jesus' statements "the Scripture cannot be annulled" (John 10:35), or "until heaven and earth pass away, not a letter, nor one stroke of a letter will pass from the law until all is accomplished" (Matt. 5:18), or the word to the Emmaus disciples encouraging them to believe "all that the prophets have declared" (Luke 24:25). How might one respond?

Jesus' Use of Scripture

Jesus is certainly affirming the trustworthiness of the prophetic message. In him the pointers in the Old Testament find fulfillment. His reference to each "jot or tittle" (KJV) or "stroke of a letter" is typical of the hyperbole he often used to make his points, such as "cut off hand," "turn the other cheek" (Matt. 6:30, 39), and more. Jesus was getting at the spirit of the law, not highlighting the letter. The Pharisees focused on the letter while missing the spirit: "You strain out a gnat, but swallow a camel," Jesus said of them in a wonderful touch of humorous irony (Matt. 23:24).

How Jesus used the Scriptures helps us to understand his appreciation of biblical authority. Some books meant a lot more to him than others. Of the thirty-nine books of the Old Testament only twenty-three are referred to by Jesus. Regarding these references only fifty-one of 122 are precise quotations. The other seventy-one convey the idea of the reference in his own words and in one instance we cannot even find the location of his, "as the Scripture has said" (John 7:38)! *For Jesus it was the message that mattered, not verbal precision.*

I was glad to learn that in 1972 Fuller Theological Seminary deleted the term *inerrancy* from its statement of faith, recognizing it to be "unreasonable, unnecessary, and misleading."[2] Fuller scholar George Eldon Ladd advocated an avenue to interpretation that followed a faith-oriented historical-critical approach with the word *theological* included. A correct interpretation thus must square with the character of God as revealed in Jesus Christ. This means Scriptural words lie under the guidance and illumination of the living Word.

See how this happens when the Scribes and Pharisees bring a woman taken in adultery to Jesus. Here "Bible-believers" challenge Jesus about his belief in the Bible. The law of Moses is clear and prescribes the death penalty for her (Lev. 20:10). We recall what Jesus does: He says nothing, bends down, and writes with his finger in the ground. Then he speaks. "Let anyone among you who is without sin be the first to throw a stone at her." Her accusers leave stunned. Then Jesus says to her, "Neither do I condemn you. Go your way, and from now on do not sin again" (John 8:1-11).

As an aside, I acknowledge that some ancient manuscripts do not include this story. Could it be that this action of Jesus so shocked even his friends that some writers were hesitant to include it?

Scriptures that do not measure up to the love, truth, and grace Christ has come to reveal are obviously not to be regarded as expressing the eternal will of God. Their place in the Bible has "time-bound cultural" significance, as Dr. E. J. Carnell used to say. Eternal truth must harmonize with the One who said: "I am the way, and the truth, and the life" (John 14:6).

The same can be shown in Jesus' treatment of the Sabbath laws as understood by his contemporaries. He felt no obligation to keep these or any other religious rules that may have kept him from showing mercy to someone in need. The biblical wisdom to which he subscribed was this word from his Father: "I desire mercy not sacrifice [ritual]" (Matt. 12:7). Jesus is Lord of the Sabbath even as he is Lord of Scripture. Both the Sabbath and the Bible have been given to us by God. Guidelines for their appreciation and use have been revealed to us by the Son of God.

Diversity of Biblical Literature

This is not the time or place to go into a lengthy dissertation of a doctrine of biblical authority, except to point out that the Bible itself does not teach us to believe that all of its contents are to be taken literalistically. This needs emphasis, since many who believe in a fiery eternal hell view Scripture as material that must be taken literally. They may not like the thought of their neighbors spending an eternity in "unquenchable fire" but feel that believing this is an ingredient of obedience to their Lord, who they feel sanctions belief in that kind of interpretation of the Bible.

Such believers have failed to appreciate the rich diversity of literary forms which God's Spirit chose to use in conveying the divine messages to us. This seems to be the case with John Blanchard, who defends the traditional teaching of an eternal hell in his recent book, *Whatever Happened to Hell?* [3]

Inconsistent Interpretations

The truth of the matter is that even fundamentalists, in fact, do not take all of the Bible literally. They claim they do; as Jerry Falwell puts it, "The Bible is the inerrant word of the living God. It is absolutely infallible, without error in all matters pertinent to faith and practice, as well as in areas such as geography, science, history, etc."[4] Yet when Jesus suggests that the man guilty of lust pluck out his eye—"tear it out and throw it away" (Matt. 5:29)—it is not taken literally. The epistles' frequent injunction to greet one another with a "holy kiss" is not practiced literally in American conservative churches. When Paul says that the gospel has been "proclaimed to every creature under heaven" (Col. 1:23) we do not expect him to mean that literally. We cannot believe Paul's reference to all Cretans as being "always liars, vicious brutes, lazy gluttons." Then he says, "That testimony is true" (Titus 1:12, 13). Really, Paul?

A laughable problem for literalists was debated by some in the early centuries of the church. When reference was made to our Lord's comment about hell, "There will be weeping and gnashing of teeth" (Matt. 24:51), an old forgery claims that for those who die toothless "teeth will be provided." Bruce Metzger tells of a friend who used to amuse others by telling them that dentures are provided in the next world so that all the damned might be able to weep and gnash their teeth.

I know Reverend W. A. Criswell wishes to defend biblical authority when he says that the Bible "is the writing of the living God. Each sentence was dictated by God's Holy Spirit."[5] But rather than honoring God, I believe such an affirmation risks robbing God of his glory.

Are we to say that Jesus was wrong when he said to his disciples as they were looking at the temple, "You see all these, do you not? Truly I tell you, not one stone will be left here upon another; all be thrown down" (Matt. 24:2). Archeologists have uncovered the awful devastation Jesus predicted, but there are parts of the walls where some stones still rest on the lower ones as originally built. The literalist must concede that Jesus erred. But when one recognizes Jesus' frequent use of hyperbole, his statement is true.

If God dictated Scripture, why is his grammar less than perfect in Mark? His numbers inconsistent where the same events are recorded in Kings and Chronicles? Women judged more harshly than men in Exodus? And why the slanderous statement made by Paul regarding Cretans? Many other such inconsistencies could be cited, as Bishop John Shelby Spong has done in *Rescuing the Bible from Fundamentalism*.[6] I will not charge God with those mistakes. Yet I can still receive God's truth through his fallible witnesses. That is the glory of divine inspiration!

We do not believe we are to follow all of the commands in the book of Exodus. We make a distinction between the "Ten Commandments" in Exodus 20 and some of the laws given in 21 and 22, such as "Whoever curses his father or mother shall be put to death" (21:17). If a slave has been beaten but "survives a day or two, there is no punishment; for the slave is the owner's property" (21:21). "You shall not permit a female sorcerer to live" (22:18). (How about a male sorcerer?)

We remember that there were zealots in New England who took that reference literally. In Salem, Massachusetts, people calling themselves Bible believers literally and shockingly acted out Exodus 22:18. This illustrates the dangers in taking all passages of the Bible literalistically, including those on hell.

Paul's statement about women keeping "silent in the churches" (1 Cor. 14:34) is another passage not taken literally by many fundamentalists. We can be grateful they don't, for in many cases women have exercised their spiritual gifts with great effectiveness in the ministry of Christ's church. In what may appear as an about-face, Paul acknowledges this in his closing greetings in Romans 16. There he commends Phoebe, a deacon (minister) of the church at Cenchreae, and several other women leaders in the churches.

Striving for Consistency

The point I want to emphasize to fellow Bible-believers is this: In many instances we are already practicing principles of interpretation that respect the limitations of language, that recognize variant literary forms, and that appreciate the role cultural context plays in getting at the true meaning of a passage.

We know the events in Genesis predate written history, so we do not expect eyewitness accuracy from an oral tradition. We recognize the Psalms as songs and prayers in poetic form. The literary form of the Gospels is mainly narrative. The epistles are apostolic letters to churches, often addressing known situations.

A very different type of writing is seen in the book of Revelation, which is written in apocalyptic imagery to announce Christ's final victory. We don't take these visions in Revelation literally, unless, of course, we are ready to meet our Lord with a two-edged sword coming out of his mouth! (Rev. 1:16). Some of course do still insist on literalizing the book of Revelation, especially its references to hell. But such an approach ignores the literary genre the Spirit chose for John to use in disclosing the ultimate triumph of God over Satan.

Much of the Bible—history, doctrinal messages, teachings, and more—ought to be taken literally. But the Scriptures include many literary forms, some of which, like poetry and allegory, cannot be understood if taken literalistically. Some of the language is figurative or metaphoric.

It is understanding we seek. If we need to wrestle with a text, study its historic and cultural context, recognize its linguistic style, so much the better. It's not all easy to understand. Peter even had trouble with some of Paul's writings (2 Pet. 3:16). But the truth is there, and certainly in all ethical issues, the closer the truth matches what we know of Jesus Christ, the closer we have come to the meaning God's Spirit intended.

Again, the biggest problem with taking the whole Bible as the verbally dictated word of God is that it puts the text of Scripture above the living Word of God, Jesus Christ. Many verses in the Bible clearly are contradicted by the manner and message of Jesus. In Leviticus a child who curses his parent is to be put to death (Lev. 20:9). Jesus does not support that form of discipline. Let Jesus be Lord of Scripture, not the reverse!

The Pharisees were believers in the inerrancy of Scripture. So when the woman taken in adultery was brought before Jesus, he was being challenged to obey the word of the Bible! Jesus smashed the tradition of literalism and forgave the woman. Later he pointed out to his followers how the letter kills, but the spirit brings life (John 6:61-63), which Paul repeats (2 Cor. 3:6). We need to keep this principle of interpretation in mind when we consider references to hell.

Mary Magdalene may well have been another candidate for stoning. After all, to be possessed by seven demons would certainly qualify her for witchhood (remember Exod. 22:18). Yet here again Jesus meets her with grace, pardons her, and later commissions her to bring the good news of his resurrection to the frightened disciples (John 20:16-18). Behold, the first woman preacher!

The Point of It

This tradition of emphasizing a literal interpretation of the Bible is what has supported the doctrine of a literal hell. Once we are freed from this restrictive tenet we will be able to recognize the passages on hell as important warning passages that teach a truth which must be taken seriously, but not literalistically. Consequences of rejecting God's grace are fearful, but the picture of sinners being roasted over an open flame for all ages belongs in the caricature section of the local tabloids, not in the doctrinal statements of Christian churches. The metaphors of fire, darkness, voracious worms, gnashing teeth, and endless anguish are intended to be shocking. Effective warnings are. The consequences of rejecting God's love and life are dismal and deadly.

The message is clear when the rights of language are honored. God is honored as the righteous Judge. The message is distorted when the words are taken literally. Then God is pictured as a sadist, which is impossible to harmonize with the God and Father of our Lord Jesus Christ.

Rejecting the Traditional View of Hell

WHEN JESUS SPOKE OF THE NEED TO "eat the flesh of the Son of man and drink his blood" to live, (John 6:53) his hearers were offended. With a pharisaic tendency toward literalism, this statement would sound almost cannibalistic. His own followers call it "difficult." It implies a total commitment, for it means taking the Lord into one's life by an action as literal as eating and drinking. Such a commitment is, of course, a matter of a person's will and spirit. Jesus, recognizing their hesitation, turns to them. "Does this offend you? It is the spirit that gives life; the flesh is useless. The words that I have spoken to you are spirit and life" (John 6:61-63).

Jesus gives us the hermeneutic tool that will guide us to proper interpretations. It has to do with the spiritual thrust of his words, many of which are metaphorical images conveying meanings far beyond the literal picture. However Christians may interpret the Holy Eucharist, they agree that this memorial feast celebrates our Lord's gracious provision of himself in meeting our need to be cleansed, filled and nourished by his risen life. "His words are spirit and life."

The Letter Kills

Paul followed his Lord in this approach. He spoke of the gospel as a ministry of a "new covenant, not of letter but of spirit; for the letter kills, but the Spirit gives life" (2 Cor. 3:6). Paul had been a literalistic Pharisee once. Now in Christ he authors the greatest passage on love in the literature of the world (1 Cor. 13). Tongues, prophetic insight, wisdom, understanding, or knowledge amount to nothing apart from love. Not even faith or benevolence are worthwhile absent love!

Paul has caught the spirit of Christ. Surely, if the love of God as revealed in Jesus Christ is recognized as the primary disclosure of the heart of God, then no Bible reference or interpretation that stands in contradiction to such love can be taken as a valid Christian doctrine. This must be remembered when an eternal hell is considered.

God's Love in Christ, The Measure

So Old Testament laws about killing children who curse their parents, or killing homosexuals, or killing sorcerers, or killing all Midianites, are not reliable guides for those who follow Christ. It is following this line of interpretation—understanding the lesser teachings in the light of the greater—that we reject the traditional view of hell.

When biblical scholars follow this line of interpretation they are criticized as violating the teaching of verbal inerrancy. But what these critics apparently are not seeing is that they are putting their doctrine of inerrancy above Christ. He is the living Word of God, and Lord of all, including the inspired book we call the Bible. We will edit, interpret, understand, and apply the Scriptures in the light of Jesus Christ. We will not change the gospel's picture of Jesus to fit, say, the book of Judges.

So more and more biblical scholars and thoughtful pastors, while still holding a high view of biblical authority, are challenging the traditional understanding of hell. Letting Jesus be their guide, they have seen his references to hell (Hades or Gehenna) as metaphoric images that warn of the serious consequences of abusing freedom as William Crockett has done.[1] Judgment is clearly taught but not, if metaphor is the intended meaning, a sadistic God.

Challenging Tradition

John Stott finds the thought of worshiping a torturing God offensive. He puts it like this: "I find the concept intolerable and do not understand how people can live with it without either cauterizing their feelings or cracking under the strain."[2] One of the best defenses of a biblical view of judgment that rejects the concept of a God of vindictive horror has been made by Clark H. Pinnock. In *Four Views On Hell*, edited by William Crockett, the "conditional view" articulated by Pinnock seems to me to be worth careful consideration. (His chapter on "Hell: Rejecting Love," was an earlier interpretation in the book he co-authored with Robert Brow on *Unbounded Love*.[3])

Here briefly is how Pinnock understands the Bible's teaching about hell. He finds it scripturally consistent to interpret hell as destruction rather than endless torture of the wicked. Rejecting God is self-destructive. He affirms the verse which reads, "the wages of sin is death" (Rom. 6:23). Pinnock believes it is time to put aside the traditional view of hell and replace it with an understanding of judgment more in keeping with the biblical picture of God as revealed in Jesus Christ.

If we are encouraged by our Lord to love our enemies, how could continuous vindictive punishment fit with this same Lord who commanded mercy from us? Pinnock writes, "Torturing people forever is an action easier to associate with Satan than with God, measured by ordinary moral standards and/or by the gospel. And what human crimes could possibly deserve everlasting torture?"[4]

Hell As Annihilation

So what could hell mean? Pinnock does not find universalism in the Bible so he opts for "annihilationism or conditional immortality." He quotes Edward Selwyn, who wrote,

> There is little in the New Testament to suggest a state of everlasting punishment, but much to indicate an ultimate destruction or dissolution of those who cannot enter into life: conditional immortality seems to be the

doctrine most consistent with the teaching of Scripture.[5]

It does seem surprising that more theologians have not picked up on this, which only serves to show how glued we can become to tradition. The Bible uses "the language of death and destruction, of ruin and perishing, when it speaks of the fate of the impenitent." "Eternal" punishment suggests an irreversible judgment by the eternal One, rather than an experience of endless torment.

Once one is open to this interpretation, it is surprising how many Scriptures fit. Psalm 37 declares that the wicked will "fade like grass" (v. 2) "be cut off and be no more" (vv. 9 and 10) "perish and vanish" (v. 20) "be destroyed" (v. 38). The best known verse among Christians describes the fate of unbelievers with the word "perish" (John 3: 16).

Jesus speaks of the possibility of "body and soul being destroyed in hell" (Matt. 10:28). The references to Gehenna could certainly imply death by its fires. Many of Paul's references seem to point to a final destruction of the wicked (2 Thess. 1:9; Gal. 6:8; 1 Cor. 3:17; Phil. 1:28). Peter also spoke of the destruction of the wicked, (2 Pet. 2:1, 3:3:7). Other New Testament passages express similar teaching.

Pinnock believes one of our problems has come from accepting the Greek notion of the soul's immortality. If this be the case, the soul must go somewhere at death. But the Bible teaches the resurrection of the person, not the eternal nature of the soul. God alone "has immortality" Paul tells Timothy (1 Tim. 6:16). Life and immortality have come through the gospel (2 Tim. 1:10). The gift of God is eternal life (John 3:16).

We were created with the capacity for life everlasting, but this is a gift of God to those who come to Him for mercy. Those who reject God's love are free to choose death. They miss the gift of eternal life. "Perish" is the word John uses for them. "Once this is seen, a person is free to read the Bible on hell naturally and straight-forwardly."[6]

Pinnock's view, however, can be challenged by first-century references to an afterlife for both the righteous and unrighteous. The parable of the rich man in hell (Luke 16:19-

31), would suggest this. Josephus, the Jewish historian of the first century, indicates that the Pharisees had endorsed the Hellenistic view of the immortality of the soul, combining it with the resurrection for both the good and the bad. Paul, once a Pharisee, no doubt shared this view, but stressed the hope of imperishable resurrection (1 Cor. 15:53).

The Moral Problem

Besides the exegetical challenges in the traditional view of hell just discussed, the moral problem is even greater. Jesus revealed a love and grace in God unparalleled in any religion or philosophy. It was so amazing, John had to write "God *is* love" (1 John 4:16). No interpretation of God that differs, challenges, or contradicts this view can be considered valid. Again I refer to Clark Pinnock's statement:

> Everlasting torture is intolerable from a moral point of view because it pictures God acting like a bloodthirsty monster who maintains an everlasting Auschwitz for his enemies whom he does not allow to die. How can one love a God like that?[7]

An eternal hell poses the problem of a glaring inconsistency in the character of God. There is an affront to an enlightened sense of justice. There is also the matter of what purpose is served by it all. Finally, the question can be raised about whose victory is finally won if most people are in hell.

The Character of God

While the Bible recognizes God as holy and therefore as requiring justice, it does not see God as being vindictive or wanting to punish. A description of God recurring in the Bible is expressed in these words:

> His anger is but for a moment; his favor is for a lifetime. Weeping may linger for the night, but joy comes with the morning. (Ps. 30:5)

> He will not always accuse nor will he keep his anger forever. He does not deal with us according to our sins, nor repay us according to our iniquities. (Ps. 103:9-10)

The New Testament portrait of God painted by Jesus is even more emphatic regarding God's mercy and grace. Ninety-nine sheep may be safe, but if one is missing the good shepherd searches until he finds that one lost sheep.

When the prodigal son is still a great way off, his father sees and runs to embrace his "once lost, now found" son. Then he assures the reluctant elder brother that "all that is mine is yours" (Luke 15:31). The more one ponders the stories of Jesus and the implications of his death and resurrection—"if while we were enemies, we were reconciled to God through the death of his Son, much more surely, having been reconciled, will we be saved by his life" (Rom. 5:10)—then we understand why "Amazing Grace" is such a popular hymn. God's grace is incredibly amazing, as Philip Yancey has so eloquently expressed it in his book *What's So Amazing About Grace?*[8]

That picture of God is incompatible with the image of a deity who would subject most of humanity to endless torture. For those who hold to a doctrine of election, the problem intensifies. What can be said about God if "from eternity he decided to send most people to eternal damnation in order that his grace toward others might appear more laudable"?[9] If eternal punishment was the goal for which most people are destined, why create them in the first place? How can the same God who commands us to love our neighbors, enemies included, ask us to concur with this endless torture?

Clark Pinnock asks, "How can one love a God like that? I suppose one might be afraid of him, but could we love and respect him? Would we want to strive to be like him in such mercilessness?"[10] Hans Küng poses the issue with this question: "What would we think of a human being who satisfied his thirst for revenge so implacably and insatiably?"[11]

Since the first and greatest command in the Bible is to give wholehearted love to God and to neighbor (Matt. 22:37), it becomes increasingly clear that the doctrine of an eternal hell stands in contradiction to this divine law. Based on this repeated biblical law, the rejection of traditional hell cannot be said to be the opinion of "soft-hearted" sentimentalists, as has often been charged. We are stressing what Jesus called first and foremost! (Mark 12:30; Luke 10:27)

However we interpret texts on judgment, our conclusions must not contradict the larger teaching about the love of God for all the world. The big picture must remain big.

The Cry for Justice

Made in the image of God, all humans have a moral sense, a judicial sentiment. Even the unredeemed cringe when the Holocaust is reviewed. Our moral intuition rejects the idea that anyone, human or divine, who endlessly inflicted pain on another, could be called "good."

Throughout history we read of religious factions and political parties justifying their cruelty to others. The Nazis justified their anti-Semitic atrocities. The Communists justified their anti-Christian murders. Early Americans justified slavery. But history has judged such violations of human rights as breaching a universal moral code. Every human has incalculable worth. Christianity affirms a double value for all people. We were created in the image of God and this Creator has also written our worth in the life blood of his only Son.

Because the human has this value and dignity, some socities are increasingly recognizing that punitive retribution may not be the most just or effective way to deal with offenders. A more enlightened approach attempts rehabilitation of lawbreakers, not simply their destruction. If this is the direction of a more humane society, do such trends not reflect more accurately the Savior who ate and drank with "tax collectors and sinners?"

In years past, cruelty and injustice may well have found support in the traditional understanding of hell. The Crusades and the Inquisition certainly did. Failing to understand that God's judgments were meant to bring about repentance, the church justified hellish actions by claiming God's name in their heinous deeds. Blindness to God's justice and mercy can only lead to terrible injustice among humans.

We often talk of "making the punishment fit the crime." The Hebrew Bible puts in terms of "eye for eye, tooth for tooth, hand for hand, wound for wound, stripe for stripe" (Exod. 21:22). This was to limit punishment. But Jesus goes further. In Matthew 5:38-48 he calls on us to "turn the other cheek," to "pray for those who persecute you." The section ends with the admonition to be "perfect as your heavenly Father is perfect" (Matt. 5:48) implying that this is the Father's loving response to those who fail to love him.

It must also be mentioned that "eternal" punishment for "temporal" sins can hardly be considered justice. Attempts to defend the traditional position fall flat when addressing this question. Understandably a holy God will not ignore sin, not only because it mars his plan but also because it hurts the creatures God loves. Yet as the prophets have spoken, the justice of God is intended to heal not destroy, even though the path toward healing may include some destruction and pain.

The appeal to justice is appropriate for a Christian with a sense of right and wrong shaped by Scripture and the Holy Spirit. As we look at all the injustice in our world we weep. If this short life is all there is, then life is an absurd tragedy.

We find hope, however, in the assurance that God is not finished with us when we die. If Christ is Lord "both of the dead and the living" (Rom. 14:9), then God's justice will still be revealed to those who missed it on earth. Peter is quite specific in affirming the ongoing action of God for those who have died. "For this reason the gospel was proclaimed even to the dead, so that, though they had been judged in the flesh as everyone is judged, they might live in the spirit as God does" (1 Pet. 4:6). How God's grace and mercy will work for people after they die, we cannot fully understand, but we can affirm that God will be just and, as always, God's justice will be immersed in mercy.

The traditional view of hell fails the test of justice.

The Point of It All

An eternal hell serves no purpose. If nothing is achieved but punishment for its own sake, then it is pointless. Surely we cannot accept the point of view that those in heaven are happier by seeing the anguish of souls in hell. This was actually taught! Thomas Aquinas stated that the saved "will, in fact, rejoice at the pains of those who are condemned. Their own bliss will be all the more enjoyable in contrast with the misfortune of the lost."[12] One is tempted to question the salvation of those who could enjoy seeing anyone suffer. What a terrible misrepresentation of our Lord.

Scripture teaches us that God has reasons for his actions, reasons prompted by wisdom and love. Yes, they go far beyond our comprehension many times (Isa. 55:8, 9), but they are never pointless. What point could be made by subjecting the majority of his creatures (or even just a few) to everlasting torment? Such an image resembles more some pagan deity than the God and Father of our Lord Jesus Christ.

Who Is Victorious?

Paul wrote to Timothy that "God our Savior desires everyone to be saved and to come to the knowledge of the truth" (1 Tim. 2:4). If this is God's will, then the traditional view of hell would spell God's defeat. Clearly that is not the teaching of the Bible. There would be no victory of God's love if most people are left screaming in the flames of hell.

Reflecting on 1 Corinthians 15:28, John Stott wonders, "How can God in any meaningful sense be called 'everything to everybody' while an unspecified number of people still continue in rebellion against him under his judgment?"[13] Stott is correct. God's purpose shall be fulfilled. An endless duality of heaven and hell is at best a tie game. That is not the message of the gospel. God in Christ has won the victory for the whole world. This is the good news!

> As I live, says the Lord, every knee
> shall bow to me,
> and every tongue shall give
> praise to God. (Rom. 14:11)

God's victory runs through Scripture. Consider a few of the verses that highlight the theme (headings added):

> *Egypt will be saved*
> The Lord will make himself known to the
> Egyptians, and the Egyptians will know the Lord

on that day. The Lord will strike Egypt, striking
and healing; they will return to the Lord and he
will listen to their supplications and heal them.
(Isa. 19:21, 22)

Sodom and Samaria will be saved
I will restore their fortunes, the fortunes of Sodom
and her daughters and the fortunes of Samaria
and her daughters. . . .
(Ezek. 16:53)

Israel will be saved
All Israel will be saved; as it is written; Out of
Zion will come the Deliverer, he will banish
ungodliness from Jacob.
(Rom. 11:26)

All nations will be saved
All the ends of the earth shall remember and
turn to the Lord; and all the families of the
nations shall worship before him.
(Psalm 22:27)

All the nations you have made shall come and
bow down before you, O Lord, and shall
glorify your name.
(Psalm 86:9)

And he (God) will destroy in this mountain the
shroud that is cast over all peoples the sheet
that is spread over all nations; he will swallow
up death forever. Then the Lord will wipe away
the tears from all faces.
(Isa. 25:7, 8)

All creation saved
The wolf shall live with the lamb, the leopard
shall lie down with the kid. . . . They will not hurt
or destroy on all my holy mountain; for the
earth will be full of the knowledge of the Lord
as the waters cover the sea.
(Isa. 11:6-9)

Creation itself will be set free from its bondage
to decay and will obtain the freedom of the glory of
the children of God.
(Rom. 8:21)

Through him God was pleased to reconcile to
himself all things, whether on earth or in heaven, by
making peace through the blood of his cross.
(Col. 1:20)

All saved
As one man's trespass led to condemnation for
all, so one man's act of righteousness leads to
justification and life for all.
(Rom. 5:18)

As all die in Adam, so shall all be made alive in
Christ . . . the last enemy to be destroyed is death. . . .
so that God may be all in all.
(1 Cor. 15:22, 26, 28)

In Christ God was reconciling the world to himself,
not counting their trespasses against them. . . .
(2 Cor. 5:19)

All this has become possible because, as John the Baptist
said in pointing to Jesus, "Here is the Lamb of God who takes
away the sin of the world!" (John 1:29). He did not die for a
few. He carried the burden of the world's sins, and he carried them away to judgment and death. "Thanks be to God,
who gives us the victory through our Lord Jesus Christ!" (1
Cor. 15:57).

That victory spells the defeat of the traditional view of
hell. There is no eternal hell if "God is all in all."

So a view of hell that is morally consistent with the character of God as revealed in Jesus Christ is the view that allows for human freedom and still maintains the love of God.
God does not want anyone to perish (2 Pet. 3:9). God does
not force us against our wills. Should we choose to reject
God's love, we are left with our rejection. To walk away from
life is to make the death choice. Heaven weeps as do all sen-

sitive people at the folly of such a choice, but Pinnock believes the justice of God then orders closure, not torture.

However, closure or annihilation still does not spare God the "killer" label. Endless torment serves no purpose, but does annihilation of most people square any better with God's purposes? It seems to me that a chastening punishment with the intention of bringing about repentance still fits best with the Father whom Jesus revealed.

Hell has been claimed as part of church dogma for centuries. Its images have at times been gross and utterly unChrist like. But the church was attempting to be faithful to Scripture. It is an awesome prospect for any of us to meet our Lord unprepared. The consequences of rejecting the abundant and eternal life offered in the gospel are deadly. In wanting to declare the folly of rejecting God's mercy, the church allowed unbiblical features to color its portrayal of hell until it became a terrible distortion of the God and Father of our Lord Jesus Christ.

By looking again at the biblical texts and seeing them in the light of Christ, we are given a view of hell that points to an execution of divine justice that leads ultimately to the full realization of God's will for all creation. Hell will have served its purpose. Everyone will finally praise the Lord! Leslie D. Weatherhead put it like this: "Always there will be the chance to turn and love and live. The nature of the soul demands it. The nature of God proclaims it. The compassion of Christ guarantees it."[14]

9

Criteria of Judgment

"I HOPE HE BURNS FOREVER IN HELL!" So said a bereaved father as they sentenced the rapist and killer of his daughter. One can understand his emotion. Time and again we hear of horrible things committed by fellow human beings and we are shocked and angered. A man pours gasoline on his wife and ignites the flames that kill her. Three white men in Texas tie a black man to the back of their pick-up and drag him to an awful death. In Wyoming a young man is tied to a fence and beaten to death because he was gay. The Nazi machine under Hitler's direction puts to death six million Jewish people. Hijackers pilot airliners into buildings. "I hope they burn forever in hell!" is the understandable reaction of hurt and anger to such atrocities.

Emotional Theology

These are emotional reactions, however, not the building blocks of a stable theology. We cannot ignore the message of such revulsion. It speaks of the judicial sentiment in people created in the image of God. We cry out for justice. But our emotional response does not provide an accurate description of what divine justice really is.

I don't remember much talk of hell when I was a kid. Occasionally it would come up. We were Mennonites and Mennonites were bound for glory. Some Lutherans might also make it, my grandpa, a Mennonite preacher, informed me.

After all, we were using Luther's translation of the Bible since our services were still in German at that time.

Bolsheviks, of course, were hell-bound. It was because of them my parents had to flee Russia. Most English-speaking folks were suspect. Roman Catholics were definitely bound for hell since the Pope was the anti-Christ. In later years when sharing these views with Catholic friends, they laughed as they told me they had been taught that Protestants are bound for perdition, especially Luther.

Thankfully those days are over, I trust. In fact, I heard one Catholic priest make the comment that the way things were moving Luther might become "one of our next saints!"

It is remarkable to note how often we declare that it's the other guy, the other race, the other political party, and the other religion. Most often those who are different from ourselves are who are bound for hell.

A mission advertisement in *Christianity Today* had this arresting headline: "By this time tomorrow 37,000 Muslims will die without Christ." By implication they were hell-bound. In thinking of our Lord we notice that he never said anything like that.

Playing God

On June 3, 1998, an esteemed senator, Barry Goldwater, was laid to rest at Trinity Cathedral in Phoenix, Arizona. That was the church where he was baptized and on the membership roll throughout his lifetime. The service itself was comforting and uplifting.

However, a negative note was played by a Baptist minister. Fred Phelps, with some members of his church in Topeka, Kansas, had decided to visit Phoenix to picket the funeral. One of their signs read, "Barry is in hell." When asked by reporter E. J. Montini of the *Arizona Republic* (which reported this vignette at the time), why they believed such a thing, the reply was, "He was a supporter of Sodomites." That was their criteria for a trip to hell. They even included the recently departed Sonny Bono because he failed "to condemn his gay daughter."

Aside from the disgrace this so-called-reverend brings to the gospel of Jesus Christ for failing to show either love or respect for those in a state of grief, his condemnations violate the command of Jesus against judging others (Matt. 7:1-5). He has usurped a role only God can fulfill. When it was pointed out to certain fundamentalists that by their reckoning only a tiny segment of humanity will make it to heaven, they did not appear too upset. They reminded me that Jesus said, "the gate is narrow and the road is hard that leads to life" (Matt. 7:14).

It is true that a full response to God's holy love is rare, even among the saints. However, most interpreters do not see this statement as a reference to final judgment. While the "numbers game" is probably beside the point of criteria for the "hell-express," one conservative preacher assured me heaven may not be as lonely as first perceived, since all aborted infants and children who die before the age of accountability will also be in heaven.

I suggested, perhaps a bit too flippantly, that then he ought to support abortionists, since this would guarantee heaven for those little ones. He didn't appreciate my sarcasm. But maybe the absurd knots this illustration suggests we can tie ourselves in ought to sober us up in regard to determining who goes where. If we are ready to leave the fate of infants and children with our heavenly Father, maybe it would be wise to leave all God's children in the hands of the One whose justice we can trust and whose grace is "amazing."

The Road Signs

Am I suggesting that there are no criteria, no road signs to indicate one or the other designation? Certainly not. There are numerous pointers. Taken alone some seem very restrictive. Taken together the picture broadens. In fact, the biblical picture is far more inclusive than fundamentalists preach. They will quickly point to a verse like "those who do not believe are condemned already, because they have not believed in the name of the only Son of God" (John 3:18). Then they will add that since the name of the Son is Jesus, this means everyone must believe in Jesus, must accept him "as personal Savior," to be saved. But such an interpretation is too narrow. It ignores many other passages that give us the larger and truer picture of how God judges.

First of all, let us remember that there is no passage in the Bible stating that on judgment day God will ask, "Did you accept Jesus as your personal Savior?" In fact, no judgment passage asks anything about the doctrines or beliefs of the individual! While salvation is by God's grace alone, it may come as a surprise to many that all judgment passages refer to our deeds, not to our professions of faith. As Klyne Snodgrass has said, Scriptures "consistently teach that judgment is according to works," on the basis of light received.[1]

This may sound like a contradiction of the well-established teaching of "justification by faith alone." Not at all! Saving faith is a reliance upon the grace of God. No thoughtful person, aware of divine standards, could possibly believe that his or her good deeds would merit salvation. It is only by the generosity of God that anyone can hope for heaven. This is the gospel promise.

However, notice how Paul completes his statement about justification by faith. He says that "it is by grace you have been saved through faith . . . for we are [God's workmanship] what he has made us, created in Christ Jesus for good works, which God prepared beforehand to be our way of life" (Eph. 2:8-10).

The idea of faith in Scripture is much more than mental assent. It has to do with a commitment that involves obedience. Jesus' invitation was "Follow me!" which turns belief into action. As for believing in his "name," Bible students remember that *name* usually refers to *character* when used for God. To live for the glory of God's name is to live in harmony with the divine will and manifest divine characteristics. So in the judgment parables of Jesus the actions that reveal the divine traits gain heaven's approval. Faithful stewardship of what has been entrusted to us gains a "well done" (Matt. 25:23). Simple acts of generosity, a little food, some water, a visit, etc. gain God's welcome (Matt. 25:34-36).

This focus on deeds continues throughout the New Testament. Jesus said, "The Son of man is to come with his angels in the glory of his Father ,then he will repay everyone *for what he has done*" (Matt. 16:27). The apostle Paul repeats this theme: "For he will repay *according to each one's deeds*: to those who by patiently doing good seek for glory and honor and immortality, he will give eternal life; while for those who are self-seeking and who obey not the truth but wickedness, there will be wrath and fury" (Rom. 2:6-8). The same point is made in the last book of the Bible: "Death and Hades gave up the dead that were in them, and *all were judged according to what they had done*" (Rev. 20:13; emph. added in each quote above).

Faith and Works

This should not surprise us. Should the vine grower not expect fruit from his vine? Jesus says the branches that are fruitless are removed (John 15:2). Paul would agree with James when he wrote, "so faith by itself, if it has no works, is dead " (James 2:17). So also in John's letter the reality of faith is confirmed by the actions of love, "love is from God, everyone who loves is born of God and knows God. Whoever does not love does not know God, for God is love" (1 John 4:7, 8). "How does God's love abide in anyone who has the world's goods and sees a brother or sister in need and yet refuses help?" (1 John 3:17).

Then John proceeds to give his readers confidence regarding the day of judgment. He puts it like this:

> God is love, and those who abide in love abide in God, and God abides in them. Love has been perfected among us in this: that we may have boldness on the day of judgment, because as he is, so are we in this world. (1 John 4:16, 17)

Those who receive and share the love of God can have confidence or "boldness" on the day of judgment. Their hope in God's grace will not be disappointed. The gospel is about love, God's love for all the world. We begin to live when we begin to actively participate in this love. The amount may be small—"two very small copper coins" (Luke 21:2)—or larger, "half my possessions, Lord I will give to the poor" (Luke 19:8); or larger yet, "they shared everything they had" (Acts 4:32).

Love will find expression or it is not love. There was very little the thief on the cross could do. But he did what he could. He admitted his own guilt and defended Jesus' innocence against the accusations of the others. Then he asked to be remembered. That was all it took. Jesus assured him that "today you will be with me in Paradise" (Luke 23:42,43).

But grace had already shown itself in Jesus' prayer for all to be forgiven (Luke 23:34). That is God's desire for everyone. When we come to God, crawling, limping, hobbling, or walking, God comes to us running with arms outstretched to embrace us as Jesus put it so marvelously in the parable of the prodigal son (Luke 15:11-32).

God Is *Way* Bigger Than Our Formulas

If the only way to avoid hell is to hear and accept a particular formula—such as to "accept Jesus as personal Savior"—why did Jesus not say so? Why did he remain so many years in the carpenter shop without doing any preaching if all around him people were going to hell? Why did he heal so many without giving them a sermon, a tract, or an invitation? Why did he prevent the Gerasene from coming with him after his healing? Why did Jesus not insist on everyone joining his group when he said, "Whoever is not against us is for us" (Mark 9:39).

Why was Jesus so restrained in his own evangelizing? Why not a world tour? Why not appear to Pilate and Herod after the resurrection? For that matter, why not confront the Emperor Nero in all the glory of his resurrected power?

Why leave the task of people's eternal destiny to the likes of Peter and Andrew, James and John, Philip and Bartholomew, Matthew and Thomas, James son of Alphaeus and Thaddaeus and Simon the Cananaean and Judas Iscariot. (Mark 3:16-19)?

Or an even more puzzling question, Why leave the awesome assignment of making an eternal difference in people's lives to characters like me, not to mention the more notorious preachers?

As a parent who loves his kids, I would never leave them in the care of known incompetents. If their only hope of graduation required that they learn Spanish, I certainly wouldn't hire a tutor who couldn't speak a word of Spanish. To suggest that God would do something similar is an insult.

God's parental love far surpasses ours. Obviously there is more to life now and later than endorsing the cliched formula. The Bible itself uses numerous descriptions of how we come into God's presence:

> He has told you, O mortal, what is good; and what does the Lord require of you but to do justice, and to love kindness, and to walk humbly with your God. (Mic. 6:8)

This emphasis of several prophets besides Micah is in no way set aside in the New Testament. Believers in Jesus Christ have a marvelous advantage in having seen the revelation of God's grace and truth most clearly in Christ. Of course, New Testament evangelism will focus on Christ, as Paul said, "If you confess with your lips that Jesus is Lord and believe in your heart that God raised him from the dead, you will be saved" (Rom. 10:9).

It is through Christ and only through Christ that people are saved (Acts 4:12). But Jesus tells us that there may be many who do not recognize him now. They feed the hungry, clothe the naked, visit the lonely and are not aware that they are serving Jesus.

Still to them the invitation is extended: it will be a joyful surprise!

> Come, you that are blessed by my Father, inherit the kingdom prepared for you from the foundation of the world; for I was hungry and you gave me food, I was thirsty and you gave me something to drink, I was a stranger and you welcomed me, I was naked and you

gave me clothing, I was sick and you took care of me, I was in prison and you visited me. (Matt. 25:34-36)

Following the Light

Jesus affirms all who follow the light they have received. "Whoever does the will of my Father in heaven is my brother and sister and mother" (Matt. 12:50).

Remember Peter's surprise at Cornelius' openness to hear the gospel, "I truly understand that God shows no partiality, but in every nation, anyone who fears him and does what is right is acceptable to him" (Acts 10:34-35). And does not John put the emphasis where his Lord put it when he writes that "everyone who loves is born of God and knows God, for God is love" (1 John 4:7, 8)?

Might it not be that all who have attempted to do what is right, yet with contrite hearts recognize their failures, will still be ushered into the presence of God with Jesus as their Savior even though heretofore they have not known him by his given name? The promise in both Old and New Testament is that "Everyone who calls on the name of the Lord shall be saved" (Acts 2:21). The semantics of that name will vary, but the Lord who saves is one and the same.

The radically new ingredient in the revelation of God in Christ was the declaration that God is our heavenly parent. Jesus called God his "abba," his father, and authorized us to do the same (Matt. 6:9). Jesus used the name *Father* for God 190 times and the apostles picked up on it, adding around seventy-five more references to God as the progenitor, protector and lover of his family of earthlings.

Those who have made a conscious entry into the family of God by a commitment to Jesus Christ enjoy a unique filial relationship with God. However, the term *Father* as used by Jesus was extended to all. Even if we choose to reject God as Father, no father worth his salt rejects the son or daughter to whom he gave life.

The son in Luke 15 rejected his father, and the father allowed him to go and experience the "hell" of the far country. But he was every bit as much his son while there as he was back in the arms of his father. What the parable illustrates and what we all know all too well is that we do have freedom of choice. God does not renege in the gift of choice because love requires freedom. In fact it is not love if not freely given.

Consequences Follow Choices

It is not difficult to show the consequences of bad choices. This is a hell that is understandable. It is a hell of our making and the logic of it is firm. Where visions of hell break down is in postulating that mortal disobedience could create an eternal hell. It's very well to say that God sends no one to hell. If we go there, we do so by our own choice.

But while we have certainly created hells on earth, we humans have not been able to create anything in the life to come. That is totally within the jurisdiction of our Creator. What we do with our options in this life will have a determining effect on our experience in the life to come, but the nature of that life is fashioned by God. According to Genesis 1:31, "God saw everything that he had made, and indeed, it was very good." That included day and night. Differences are part of a varied creation. It will make a difference how we have lived.

Formula evangelism has no doubt produced some great and lasting fruit. I favor every approach that brings people into a living relationship with their God. But as George Barna has pointed out in a reporting on a pertinent poll, most people who make decisions for Christ in the formula manner (i.e. "accept Jesus as personal Savior") drop out of church participation within six to eight weeks.

Barna goes on to point out that evangelicals do not live much differently from other Americans when it comes to ethical or lifestyle choices. Their divorce rate is even higher![2] Now if God judges us all by our fruit and not by our profession of faith, maybe we need to consider more seriously what it really means to be the people of God.

What it boils down to, it seems, is the human responsiveness to light received. The Psalmist said, "in your light we see light" (Psalm 36:96). John added, "The true light, which enlightens *everyone*, was coming into the world" (John 1:9). "If we walk in the light as he himself is in the light, we have fellowship with one another, and the blood of Jesus his Son cleanses us from all sin" (1 John 1:7). The criterion of judgment is based on light received. As Leon Morris puts it, "People are judged by the light they have, not by the light they don't have."[3] This satisfies our yearning for justice and encourages trust in the One who weighs every soul with both justice and mercy.

Amazing Grace

When your heart has been touched by God's love, you want everyone to experience that same joy of being accepted, forgiven, cleansed, recreated, and blessed. You even hold out hope for some of the worst criminals. If a human could feel such longing, could we expect God to feel less?

Maybe, in the final analysis, it is this deep hunger for God to put things right that opens the door to salvation. Maybe it is this thirst for the waters of life that we crave so much, especially when we experience the dryness of evil in our world. Jesus promises a "filling for those who hungered and thirsted for righteousness." (Matt. 5:6) That promise is repeated in the Bible's final invitation to all:

> The Spirit and the bride say, "Come" and let everyone who hears say, "Come." And let everyone who is thirsty come. Let anyone who wishes take the water of life as a gift. (Rev. 22:17)

It sounds like amazing grace, doesn't it? I believe in this amazing grace for all people, but many fear this opening of the door to everyone.

Is God Limited by Time?

It has often been asserted by both Catholic and Protestant theologians that our decisions in this life determine our final destiny. To choose Christ is to choose life and heaven. To reject him is to choose death and hell. We all have freedom of choice. God saves no persons against their will. Since

God coerces none, hell is the consequence of the rebellious choice.

Does this not imply that God can only work with us while we live on planet Earth? If no possibility for any change can exist after we die, why did Jesus preach the good news to those who had died many years earlier (1 Pet. 3:19; 4:6)? Paul affirms that Christ is Lord of both "the living and the dead" (Rom. 14:9). Are we saying his lordship can have no effect on the departed?

Think about it. Some people live two years, some twenty, a few one hundred. Some have heard the good news, most have not. Some have rejected the Christ they have heard of because he seems foreign to their culture. Some rejected the message because the messenger ruined the story by his own inconsistencies. Some rejected the message because it presented Christ as the "white Western capitalist." Some have rejected the message because it seemed anti-intellectual and anti-scientific, and they felt a commitment to truth. Some rejections would be applauded by the prophets and Jesus himself when judged by the ethics of the kingdom of God. Then there are the millions who have never heard about the grace of God as revealed in Jesus Christ. It would certainly appear to be the height of injustice to condemn all these folks to hell.

Maybe a better option is to recognize that God still has much saving work to do for the millions who have departed this earth without a personal knowledge of Christ. Why must we limit God's ability to save to the brief (for many, very brief) span of time spent on earth? To do so pictures God as both unjust and extremely limited. Because only a few verses of Scripture support this possibility is no reason to reject it.

Who can say God's saving grace has run out for us when we die? If, as Peter believed, "the gospel was proclaimed even to the dead, so that . . . they might live in the spirit as God does" (1 Pet. 4:6), why not hold open this hope for all? Is this not why Christ conquered death for everyone?

There is no implication here of divine coercion on the one hand, or loss of freedom on the other. It simply underscores the fact that we dare not limit our God. If God does not wish for a single person to be lost (2 Pet. 3:9), then obviously as the teachings of Jesus make clear, God does not give up on us easily. If the flock numbers one hundred, it must always be one hundred. One sheep gone astray is not left to be lost forever. The shepherd searches until the lost one is found (Matt. 18:12-14). If ten coins is the full amount and one gets lost, the search continues until the lost is found (Luke 15:8-10). In the next parable, we see that the father's joy is not complete until his lost son comes home (Luke 15:11-32). This is what grace is all about.

Some of our young people are seen with T-shirts with the inscription: "Be patient . . . God isn't finished with me yet." Maybe God is not finished with any of us yet. If he is Lord of both the living and the dead, then can we not hope that his saving work goes on after death? Certainly, a clearer picture of Christ in judgment and grace will prove highly convincing. Someday all will see him, some for the first time. Those of us whom he has met already, know of his lavish generosity and therefore extend hope for all.

The Old Argument Rebuffed

An often repeated argument against the teaching of a final salvation for all is expressed by Erwin W. Lutzer, who has written that "Obviously, if this teaching were true there would be no pressing reason to fulfill the great commission or to urge unbelievers to accept Christ in this life."[4]

I am surprised by such a statement. The author knows "the pressing reason to fulfill the great commission" is the command of Jesus, not the prospect of hell for unbelievers. Whether hell is real is irrelevant to the disciple-making task. When Jesus issues the call to "make disciples of all nations," that is the totally sufficient reason to share the gospel.

Second, the disciple-making assignments included teaching the full message of Jesus, which does include references to some form of hell, as an expression of divine judgment. Even a moment of divine displeasure would be reason enough to be cautious about the choices we make. It could feel like eternity! Warning is part of the message.

Yet third, it needs to be noted that Jesus never placed the fear of hell in the role of motivator for disciple-making. It is absent from his calling of each disciple and absent from the great commission. The disciples were called to be salt and light in *this* needy world. They and we are called to make the love of God visible. This is the role of the church "which is his body, the fullness of him who fills all in all" (Eph. 1:22, 23). The relevance of the gospel has to do with NOW!

Fourth, if this present darkness is not sufficient motivation for proclaiming the gospel, then we must be spiritually dead. Jesus has called us to give tangible expression of his love to neighbor and enemy alike. Love will include warning people of consequences which may follow actions today or tomorrow. But if we fail to demonstrate the love of God by our deeds today, we invalidate our talk of consequences tomorrow. Our task has a present-day urgency about it.

Paul felt constrained by the love of Christ. As ambassadors for Christ, we are called to "entreat" folks to be reconciled to God (2 Cor. 5:20). We are nowhere told to threaten people with hell-fire if they fail to believe. Paul never did, nor do we read of any other disciples making such threats.

Finally, I affirm that the call to make disciples will be more effective when the picture of God is more consistent with the revelation of his Son. Many thoughtful and sensitive people have been turned away from the gospel by the narrow-minded preaching of hell fire and brimstone. "What kind of God is that?" they ask. It is not a rejection of God's holiness or justice. It is a rejection of cruelty.

Russian theologian Nicholas Berdyaev once wrote, "I can conceive of no more powerful and irrefutable argument in favor of atheism than the eternal torments of hell."[5] It is claimed that Nietzsche, Marx, and Lenin are among those whose revolt against the establishment and the church was in part based on the teaching of hell. Evangelism does better with a presentation of the God Jesus revealed as the Father of grace and love. This is the God I want to follow and will present to others.

10

About the Ultimate Future

Y ES, THE BIBLE TEACHES A JUDGMENT DAY. Life teaches us about judgment every day as consequences follow our choices. Direction determines destiny. Moving away from light can only increase the darkness. The reverse bathes us in increasing light. The logic is unassailable. To this both Bible believers and agnostics agree.

Yes, the Scriptures describe this harvest principle in terms of heaven and hell. We are all accountable. Made by God, in God's image, there is a legitimate expectation that we live up to our calling. Loving our Creator and each sister and brother enables us to fulfill the divine plan—the plan which is best for all. Spoiling that plan introduces hell. Keeping it moves us heavenward.

Yes, our Creator is also our Judge. God alone knows not only what we have done but why. God knows all about our gene pool and environmental influences. God alone knows the thoughts and intents of the heart. Therefore, only God can make the appropriate judgment. And God will.

Yes, our God is our Judge, but our Judge is also our Father. Jesus invited all to call on their Maker as their Father. Not only did he startle his contemporaries by calling God his own "Abba," he invited us all to pray "our Father" (Matt. 6:9). If God is our Father, we are the loved children of God.

The Father's will is that none of his children perish (2 Pet. 3:9). Jesus taught us to pray that the Father's will be done.

So eager was God to express this love for us all he sent his Son to rescue us from the grip of evil. In Jesus, God makes the unique, unprecedented, unrepeatable identity with all of us, in our weakness and sin. In Jesus God goes all the way to death and judgment for us that we might experience life and acceptance in him (2 Cor. 5:21). It is said he carried the sins of the world upon him (John 1:29). His resurrection tells us he left that sin-heap in the tomb. Sins belong with death.

While on that cross to accomplish this mission, Jesus prayed, "Father forgive them; for they do not know what they are doing" (Luke 23:34). Did the Father hear his Son's prayer for us all? Who will doubt it? Of course, God heard and answered with a resounding YES!

It was a "yes" for the living and a "yes" for the departed as well. Peter says that Christ suffered for sins "once for all, the righteous for the unrighteous to bring you to God. He was put to death in the flesh, but made alive in the spirit in which also he went and made a proclamation to the spirits in prison" (1 Pet. 3:18,19). Commentators differ widely in their interpretation of this passage. Is this the harrowing of hell the ancients hoped for? We cannot be sure. But Peter makes a bolder statement when he says, "For this reason the gospel was proclaimed even to the dead, so that though they had been judged in the flesh as everyone is judged, *they might live in the spirit as God does*" (1 Pet. 4:6, emph. added). Good news even for those who have died and been judged!

While commentators have struggled with the precise meaning of this verse, Peter may be saying that all are judged by death itself, but even death does not keep Jesus from extending grace to the departed. The gospel is always about grace and it is this gospel ("good news") which Peter says is proclaimed. This is the word Jesus brings to the dead, so they might "live in the spirit as God does" which obviously does not mean a place of endless torment. Pondering the possibility of this final rescue William Barclay said that "in some ways this is one of the most wonderful verses in the Bible."[1]

It is fascinating to read this verse in the letter by Peter to whom Jesus said, "You are Peter and on this rock I will build my church and the gates of Hades (hell) will not prevail against it" (Matt. 16:18). Even Hades' gates cannot keep out our sin-conquering Lord! This is what some of our Catholic friends celebrate on what they call Holy Saturday.

Hear what Eugene Peterson found in this arresting excerpt from a sermon for Holy Saturday in the Catholic Liturgy of the Hours. He quotes it in his book, *Under the Unpredictable Plant*, in a chapter on Jonah's crisis in the belly of the fish. Hear the message of Jesus in the "belly of the earth":

> God has died in the flesh and hell trembles with fear. He has gone to search for our first parent, as for a lost sheep. Greatly desiring to visit those who live in darkness and in the shadow of death, he has gone to free from sorrow the captives Adam and Eve, he who is both God and the son of Eve. The Lord approaches them bearing the cross, the weapon that had won him the victory. At the sight of him Adam, the first man he had created, struck his breast in terror and cried out to everyone: "My Lord be with you all." Christ answered him, "And with your spirit." He took him by the hand and raised him up, saying: "Awake O sleeper, and rise from the dead, and Christ will give you light."[2]

It is this passage from Peter and Paul's reference in Ephesians 4:8-10 that inspired the writer of the Apostles' Creed to include the phrase, "He descended into hell."

Even before the final formulation of this creedal statement, there was much discussion about the meaning of Christ's descent. Clement of Alexandria (150-210), a brilliant pagan-turned-Christian, was one of the first to integrate Christ's descent into Hades as part of the act of redemption. It was seen as God's way of communicating the good news to the millions who had died before the incarnation of Christ. While differences of opinion existed among students of the New Testament, Clement opted for the salvation of all the just, Jew or Gentile, and he even "suspected that in time, Satan himself might be saved."[3]

Origen, a student of Clement, further developed profound arguments for the teaching of a universal salvation.

Those texts from Peter and Paul and John's reference in Revelation 1:18, where the glorified Christ says, "I have the keys of Death and Hades," all suggested to these early Christians that there had been a "harrowing of Hell" by the victorious Christ.

Fredrick Buchner expands this theme with these arresting comments:

> "He descended into Hell," is the way the apostles' Creed puts it, of course. It has an almost blasphemous thud to it, sandwiched there between the muffled drums of "was crucified, dead, and buried" and the trumpet blast of "the third day he rose again from the dead." Christ of all people, in Hell of all places! It strains the imagination to picture it, the Light of the World making his way through the terrible dark to save whatever ones he can. Yet in view of what he'd seen of the world during his last few days in the thick of it, maybe the transition wasn't as hard as you might think.
>
> The fancifulness of the picture gives way to what seems, the more you turn it over in your mind, the inevitability of it. Of course, that is where he would have gone. Of course, that is what he would have done. Christ is always descending and re-descending into Hell.
>
> He is talking not just to other people when he says you must be prepared to forgive not seven times but seventy times seven, and "Come unto me, all ye that labor and are heavy laden" is spoken to all, whatever they've done or left undone, whichever side of the grace their Hell happens to be on.[4]

Maybe the punishment of hell is the chastening of our loving heavenly Father (Heb. 12:6). Maybe annihilation is not the ultimate outcome. Made in the image of God, our destiny is with our eternal God. Maybe the death result of sin is the hell from which the risen Lord will also awaken us. Maybe Elton Trueblood, writing about the humor of Christ, scored a bull's-eye when he said,

> The consequences of Christ's rejection of the dismal are great, not only for common life, but also for theology.

If Christ laughed a great deal, as the evidence shows, and if He is what He claimed to be, we cannot avoid the logical conclusions that there is laughter and gaiety in the heart of God. The deepest conviction of all Christian theology is the affirmation that the God of all the world is like Jesus Christ. Because the logical development is from the relatively known to the relatively unknown, the procedure is not from God to Christ, but from Christ to God. If we take this seriously we conclude that God cannot be cruel, or self-centered or vindictive, or even lacking in humor.[5]

The God and Father of our Lord Jesus Christ cannot be vindictive. The smile on our Lord's face when he rose from the dead brought incredible joy to his followers. They knew, and we must surely also know, that if the joy of the Lord was present in Jesus while accomplishing the most horrendous assignment this earth has ever seen, then he must know something wonderful still hidden from our eyes. Does this not give us reason to hope? Paul assures us we can. "May the God of hope fill you with all joy and peace in believing, so that you may abound in hope by the power of the Holy Spirit" (Rom. 15:13).

If any conclusions can be drawn from this study they surely must include these two. The first is the reality of judgment. For the rejecters of God's love and grace, appearing before the bar of divine justice will be an "experience of hell." Paul puts it like this: "for those who are self-seeking and who obey not the truth, but wickedness, there will be wrath and fury" (Rom. 2:8). Joseph Stalin will face a different verdict from that of Mother Theresa. We will "all appear before the judgment seat of Christ." The details of God's sentence are beyond our knowledge, but one cannot foresee joy among those who reject the Creator of life on that day.

The second reality has to do with the infinite greatness of God's love. Allowing Christ to be our key to biblical interpretation, we understand Scripture best when seen in his light. In fact, no teaching ought to be called Christian that does not harmonize with the character and message of Jesus.

He revealed that "God is love" (1 John 4:16), not that "God is wrath." This was also the essential message of the prophets in the Hebrew Bible. Love is everlasting (Jer. 31:3;) God's anger is a transient expression, a momentary judgment. Remember how the psalmist put it:

> For his anger is but for a moment;
> his favor is for a lifetime.
> Weeping may linger for the night,
> but joy comes with the morning. (Ps. 30:5)

When anger is recognized as "an aspect of the divine pathos," as Abraham Heschel puts it, we can understand it as instrumental—its intent is to chasten, to cleanse, to bring about repentance, and ultimately to redeem. As Heschel observes, "Its purpose and consummation is its own disappearance."[6]

Therefore, hell cannot be understood as an eternal torture chamber. No godly purpose could be served by such a sentence. "There can be no 'victory' worth the name when any of the children created and loved by God are finally defeated by a literal Hell."[7] Such would imply that Satan and the world had won. I therefore agree with the great Scottish Bible scholar, William Barclay who wrote that "in the end all persons will be gathered into the love of God."[8] Paul seems to be saying the same thing when he affirms that some day, after death itself is destroyed, God will be "all in all" (1Cor. 15:28).

So the Bible teaches a judgment. Because God is the judge it will be just. But grace is greater than judgment. "Grace that is greater than all our sin," states the hymn writer. Judgment will prevail only until its purposes have been fulfilled. The love of God will prevail forever.

I wondered where this study would take me when I began. I had no preconceived answers I intended to prove. Looking over my first draft, my friend Wesley Nelson challenged me to offer some answers, not just protest the distortions of hell as expressed by some. His advice was sound.

Here is where I now stand. I believe in both heaven and hell. I do not believe they are equally balanced opposites going on forever. Such would suggest a Zoroastrian dualism, a tie game between God and the devil. Emphatically, NO! The darkness can never overcome the light!

Hell, then, refers to that severe realm of judgment which continues until God's purposes are realized. To the God-rejecter, that may seem like an eternity. However, such a person is included in the love of God as demonstrated in the atoning sacrifice of Jesus for the sins of the whole world.

Heaven is being in the presence of our Creator and Savior, fully alive in divine light and love. This is what eternity is all about. To refer to afterlife in terms of length of days is futile, since time will be no more. The essence of heaven is living in unobstructed fellowship with God where all work and play are guided by the light of God's perfect will.

If hell is pictured as endless days of punishment for the wicked, then it would seem God's purposes have failed and Christ's victory is hollow. But this is unbiblical. God is no failure! Judgment is not the last word. Even as God's love overcame all evil on the cross of Christ, so God's will for the salvation of everyone will be realized (1 Tim. 2:4).

The verses which teach judgment must be accepted beside the verses which teach ultimate salvation for all. Klyne Snodgrass quotes the book of Ecclesiasticus from the Apocrypha which states, "Look at all the works of the Most High, they go in pairs, one the opposite of the other." He uses this quotation to prepare his readers for the tensions that permeate our faith.

In his book *Between Two Truths*, Snodgrass says, "Every truth we know is balanced by another truth that seems to be moving in the opposite direction." He refers to "faith and works," "grace and law" and others. I am proposing that we accept the tension of both judgment and salvation for all. "We will all stand before the judgment seat of Christ" (Rom. 14:10).[9]

Those who have been the recipients of grace, and have shared it, will be justified and glorified. Is it not possible that those who rejected God's grace will be condemned to the hell of remorse and the fires of regret "until" they repent?

Then they too would join in heaven's song when "every tongue shall give praise to God" (Rom. 14:11). That will be glory! It seems to me nothing less could fulfill the purposes of God's love as expressed on Calvary.

The big picture which the Bible paints is of a day when God will make all things new. It will be a new creation when death itself is destroyed and God "is all in all" (1 Cor. 15:28). So whatever else hell may be it cannot be "eternal." To say so is to degrade the victory of God in Christ.

You have heard the expression about the short-sighted person who "cannot see the forest for the trees." Many conservative interpreters have focused on their "verse-trees" in support of a literal eternal hell and have missed the far bigger picture of a glorious forest in which the righteousness and love of God flourish forever.

Therefore, I choose to hope. Being blessed by the grace of our risen Lord how can we not be filled with hope? Paul sings it out again to the Philippians in what is believed to be an early Christian hymn:

> Therefore God also highly exalted him and gave him the name that is above every name, so that at the name of Jesus every knee should bend, in heaven and on earth and under the earth, and every tongue should confess that Jesus Christ is Lord, to the glory of God the Father. (Phil. 2:9-11)

Such a confession is not made from hell!

Yes, the angels of Bethlehem had it right. God's Word in Christ is "good news of great joy for *all* the people: to you is born this day in the city of David a Savior, who is the Messiah, the Lord" (Luke 2:10, 11, emph. added).

Can anyone who hears this heavenly song not choose to hope?

> God is eternal,
> Satan is not.
> Love is eternal,
> Evil is not.
> Light is eternal,

Darkness is not.
Joy is eternal,
Misery is not.
Heaven is eternal,
Hell is not.
—*Randy Klassen*

Responses

Linford Stutzman, Nancy Heisey,
Delores Friesen, and Peter J. Dyck

Accommodating Hell to Contemporary Culture?

Why did Jesus, the authentic witness, the "true image of the Father," the consummate communicator within his cultural context, talk so freely about hell, judgment, fire? Why didn't he leave hell vague and shadowy as it was in the Old Testament, so his followers at the beginning of the twenty-first century, at the very least, would not be left with the embarrassing problem of a graphic hell?

Klassen's study is a courageous endeavor to do what seems impossible. He seeks to be faithful to the biblical material on hell and judgment. He is concerned about faithfully communicating God's revelation in Jesus within a culture that has highly developed concepts of justice to which God must conform to be attractive. He wrestles with the challenge of sharing the good news of God's love while the "bad news" of judgment lurks in the background.

While the result is a most helpful apologetic for God's love and justice within our cultural framework, it is also a demonstration of the persistent power of contemporary culture to pressure the individual's and the church's hermeneutical process to conform to cultural consensus about definitions of love and justice.

Klassen is clearly aware both of his own biases and the cultural conformity of the church's theology and practices in the past. However, as he appropriately wrestles with the traditional view of hell, his explicit awareness of the current cultural accommodation by Christians seems to be limited to the accommodation by evangelicals on the conservative end of the theological spectrum. The possibility of a more liberalizing cultural conformity by Christians within a successful, tolerant, pluralistic, morally self-satisfied culture seems to be a problem with which Klassen does not even dance, let alone wrestle. What significance hell holds for the mission of the church within this liberalizing culture is also of deep concern.

The two major areas then that need to be addressed are these: first, the pressure to accommodate Jesus' portrait of God to contemporary cultural concepts of love and justice; second, what effects this accommodation has on the mission of the church within that culture.

Cultural accommodation

There is the problem of Western culture's definitions of both love and justice. Love is seen to stand in some kind of contrast to judgment. Klassen leaves the definition of judgment open. Could God's judgment be fearsome and awful and full of grace at the same time? Could we equate truth with justice? Could we understand Jesus to be full of grace and justice? Contemporary cultural concepts of justice, played out in media trials where images, popular opinion, passion, and partial facts replace truth and objectivity, should demonstrate the inadequacy of judging God's justice. We do not know enough. Things will look different when we do.

To believe in and represent the God of Jesus, who, even with Jesus doing the revealing, does not fit with the popular, pagan definitions of goodness is problematic. Thus using an allegorical argument in relation to hell seems to make sense. But questions still remain. Why do we allegorize Jesus' language of death and judgment but not his language of life and blessing?

Culture often defines life and death wrongly. Pagan understandings, whether in the first or twenty-first centuries, differ from biblical understandings. "There is a way that seems right, but the end is the way of death." It is against a background of the reality of death and judgment that life and forgiveness in Jesus stands in contrast.

It is difficult to remain bothered by the conundrum of a loving God who *alone* has the right to judge and condemn evil. Cultural understandings of justice and love, applied to God, push Christians to reinterpret Scripture to fit these understandings. We want a God we can understand, who fits into our categories. We do not like unsolved questions. But we need to keep wrestling, not just with traditional views, but with cultural answers. We need to stay bothered.

Motivation for mission

Statistics provide a challenge to Klassen's contention that a sense of urgent concern for the eternal condition of the lost is not a necessary motivation of mission. Currently, at least seventy-five percent of all Western Protestant mission personnel and financial resources are from Baptists, Evangelicals, and Pentecostals. These are groups which, while perhaps emphasizing everything from euphoric eschatology to hell-fire damnation in their theology and witness, generally share a more traditional view of hell and judgment than the theologically more moderate and liberal mainline Protestant groups.

In addition, and contrary to what we might expect on the basis of Klassen's argument, church growth patterns around the world, including within Western culture, demonstrate this: the more conservative Christian groups continue to be more effective in their disciple-making mission efforts than mainline Protestant groups. The latter may be more inclined to interpret God's justice to avoid offense within a self-righteous culture. Jesus did not come to call the righteous, but sinners, to repentance. Sinners are who understand justice and respond to grace.

Conclusion

While my own biases and desire to communicate an attractive God within contemporary culture are very close, I suspect, to those of Randy Klassen's, it is the shocking and strange word of the gospel revealed in Jesus with which we must continue to wrestle. But we also need to wrestle with a self-righteous culture that not only is alienated from God but demands one compatible with its own presuppositions. The cross is still a stumbling block, still foolishness within religious/pagan Western culture.

Jesus' followers need to faithfully represent Jesus and the good news of the kingdom of God. We need to let Jesus' words of grace and truth speak with power and authority. For we do not know everything, and in the end Jesus will have the final word.

—Linford Stutzman, Harrisonburg, Virginia, is Assistant Professor of Mission and Culture, Eastern Mennonite University, and directs the John Coffman Center of Church Planting and Evangelism at Eastern Mennonite Seminary.

Hell and How to Read the Bible

Readers who choose to read a book about hell are likely to belong to one of two groups—either those who seek support for the idea of never-ending punishment because it helps them make sense of the obvious evil in our world, or those who are troubled by the picture of God that emerges from the idea of eternal suffering. This book, while it speaks to both of those categories of questions, is as much about how to read the Bible as it is about the concept of hell. Randy Klassen models an approach to taking the Bible seriously yet never explicitly describes a theory of interpretation behind his study.

Beginning with a survey of the biblical canon, Klassen interestingly chooses Acts as a point of entry rather than either the Hebrew Bible or the Gospels. He makes this move because he sees Acts as offering insights into the subject matter of early Christian preaching. Creatively building on that foundation, he ties the Christian proclamation to its sources in the Hebrew Bible and in the life, teachings, death, and resurrection of Jesus Christ. Klassen correctly argues that the Hebrew Bible has no concept of hell, then he turns to the Gospels to recognize the metaphorical quality of much of Jesus' teaching. When he finally addresses the epistles, Klassen underlines their emphasis on God's judgment, an emphasis that drew heavily on the theology of the Hebrew prophets.

What caught my attention throughout this book were the many references to the problem of "literalistic" interpretation of the Bible, whatever portion Klassen was considering. Over and over again as a teacher, I hear the impatient or worried question, "Why can't I just read the Bible for what it says?" Those who pose this question are usually thinking of a "literal" meaning that assumes the words on the biblical page are clear, straightforward, and without nuance.

What these readers have not considered is that they are reading a translation from another language, of a writing for which we have no original manuscript(s). Thus the matter of establishing the best possible text from which to translate, as well as questions of lexicography and syntax, lie behind whatever translation of the English Bible they read. Further, the biblical texts come from an ancient time in which the worldviews of its writers were markedly different from our own, as were in all likelihood their cultural contexts and their socio-economic class.

Others, usually biblical scholars, have proposed a different meaning for the "literal" reading of the biblical text—that is, as New Testament scholar Sandra Schneiders puts it, "what the author intended to convey."[1] The search for such information has become part of much recent biblical exegesis. Yet this understanding too presents a problem—for even if a biblical author were writing in our own time and within our own cultural context, we are never able to enter that author's mind to ferret out the intent of his or her work.

Most writing, with the exception of documents such as instruction manuals, has metaphorical qualities—that is, it "carries the reader across" from one place to another, from one level of thought to another. The biblical writings in general, as well as in their descriptions of hell, as Klassen understands, belong within the realm of metaphor. Klassen refers at several points to allegorical readings of early Christians as one way to approach the interpretation of such texts.

The question that follows is what criteria can be established for determining which interpretations are valid and which are not. Schneiders insists that no single "correct" interpretation exists, because different readers and different reading settings contribute to shaping interpretation. She proposes, however, both a negative and a positive evaluative principle for biblical interpretation.

Negatively, some approaches must be ruled out because they attempt the impossible. For example, the poetry of the Psalms does not provide scientific data. Klassen appears to appeal to a similar rule when he points out the diversity of biblical forms, or as a literary critic might call them, the different genres of the Bible (75).

As a positive criterion for biblical interpretation, Schneiders offers the question: Is the interpretation "fruitful"?[2] Again, Klassen's work uses a similar term, "usefulness," to describe the basis of the Scripture's authority (73).

I suggest that Klassen's study of what the Bible says about hell is "fruitful" in at least three ways. First, it bears evangelical fruit. The desire to help people hear as "good news" the invitation to join the Christian faith community and to follow Jesus Christ was central as he began the exploration of this book's topic.

Second, this book bears theological fruit. An understanding of God that is "in harmony with Jesus Christ" emerges from the perspective he offers (18).

Third, Klassen's work bears ethical fruit. His careful weaving together of the biblical teaching that human deeds are indeed judged with the understanding that eternal torment "fails the test of justice" (87, 95) provides a window through which to better view how God deals with evil.

Thus this book resourcefully speaks to the fundamental questions that quite likely will draw readers to it, and in the

process shows us all how serious and useful biblical interpretation can be done.

—*Nancy R. Heisey is Associate Professor of Biblical Studies
and Church History at Eastern Mennonite University and
president-elect of Mennonite World Conference.*

What About Hell on Earth?

Randy Klassen has clearly and succinctly delineated biblical references and interpretations of the various references
to hell, Gehenna, or Hades without becoming sidetracked by
current debates about end times, Armageddon, or capital
punishment. His straightforward presentation of how the
concept of hell is developed and used through both the Old
and New Testaments is the strength of the book, and this
alone should make it a great resource for readers, students,
and pastors.

Klassen has also been able to summarize the primary historical arguments and theological debates in a clear and useful way. The succinct reviews of current literature and theological positions are another gift he offers. He has been thorough without overwhelming the reader with unnecessary
detail. References are current and easy to follow and use.

Klassen's conclusions about the potential for something
approaching universal salvation or what happens after
death, however, seem less clear and potentially less biblical
to me. I find myself not sure how some of his leaps are made.
Does a belief in a loving, just, and gracious God also inevitably mean there is no ultimate separation from God?
Who gets a second chance? What then, in the end, is the definition and purpose of judgment?

In addition, what does judgment here on earth involve?
Klassen's careful study and presentation of Biblical teachings on hell focuses primarily on what happens after death
rather than how human beings face the evils, the fears, and
the private and public manifestations of punishment and
separation from God that we experience in life itself.

As a therapist and a professor of pastoral counseling, I
often find myself wrestling not with the hell or judgment that

evolves after death but the very real experiences of suffering and hell that come to people as a result of their own or others' wrongdoing. When one works with children who have witnessed drive-by shootings or murders, or listens to troubled couples vent their bitter anger, rage, and disappointment, it is easy to blame both God and human beings for the sorry state of affairs. And when the client is a victim of abuse, rape, neglect, or injustice, it is far easier to plead "Maranatha" and leave all the sorting out to God than to gird up one's loins to walk through the fire and face the valley of the shadow with the victim. Receiving and offering forgiveness helps to restore and heal. Still there is the day-by-day life to be lived and a process of working through trauma that "hurts like hell." Indeed when one is grieving, hating, or barely surviving, life often feels like a living hell.

As a professor and mentor, I work to keep faith and hope alive for myself and my students. I work especially hard at this as they grapple with the pain and suffering of the world in new ways: as they make that first child abuse report, live through someone's attempted suicide, or find themselves needing to face the darkness within themselves as they do the work necessary to become a healer. It is a challenge every day to find God's grace sufficient for the questions, needs, and concerns of each student and his or her clients. When the pastors who take my classes wrestle with the demands on their time and the needs of the people they serve, it is easy to long for a clear, unmistakable word from God that would show them the way to go, the words to say, the sermons to preach that will cause people to change and good to triumph over evil.

Earlier this year, my husband Stan and I spent several months surveying what the church, government, health care, non-governmental agencies, and missions are doing to respond to the HIV/AIDS pandemic in Africa. Since a one-semester sabbatical allowed only short visits to ten countries, we only began to see the tip of the firestorm raging in West, South, and East Africa: more than 12 million orphans; in some countries up to thirty percent of the population HIV-

infected; stigma, isolation, poverty, destruction of the infra-
structure, lack of medical care; proliferation of street children
and prostitution to ward off starvation. And if what we were
told and have read is correct, only ten percent of the dying
has happened, so there could be nine times the present
amount of misery yet to come.

Surely this is a disaster, an evil nearly unprecedented in
human history. It causes us to shudder to think what we
would have seen and felt had we been focusing on the problem, instead of on the islands of hope, love, care, education,
and healing where ministry was taking place. Many times
we were asked, "Who caused this pandemic?" "Where did it
come from?" "How do we now live out our faith amid this
terror?"

That might once have seemed too graphic a picture, but
in light of the reduction to ashes of three thousand innocent
persons, and the evaporation of two magnificent modern-
day Towers of Babel, not to mention part of the Pentagon, it
is not that hard to imagine a worldwide hell of recrimina-
tion, hate crimes, and war that could make even the Holocaust and Hiroshima look small by comparison. It is times
like these that "try men's [and women's] souls" and send us
back to the Good Book to see how God expects us "to live
and walk by faith, not sight." When leaders, photographs,
banners, editorials, and newspaper headlines ask us to consider why terrorism happens, what we did to deserve it, and
how we might stop it, one is glad there is a God who as righteous judge brings justice to the earth.

Surely Klassen cannot be expected, any more than the
rest of us in these trying and complex times, to provide a
comprehensive vision of how God judges not only after
death but also here on earth. Yet passages leap out with insights one wishes he would further develop. For example,
Klassen observes that "it may come as a surprise to many
that *all* judgment passages refer to our deeds, not to our profession of faith" (p. 95). "Rejecting God is self-destructive"
(p. 82). Or, "If we are ready to leave the fate of infants and
children with our heavenly Father, maybe it would be wise

to leave all God's children in the hands of the One whose justice we can trust and whose grace is 'amazing'" (p. 94).

My clients, my students, and I live every day with the tragic consequences of sin, including darkness and ongoing torment that sometimes seems as if it will never end. After the September 11, 2001 attacks, thousands more entered great suffering and it appears all too possible that still more, in our country and in other nations, will experience it. I agree with Klassen that self-destructive behaviors almost always have their root in rejection of God, but what about those that come from the pain of being rejected or traumatized by others? This latter question seems underexplored in the book. Christians would do well to discuss and recognize when and how we bring destruction into our own world and into the world of others.

Maybe one point of the Bible's teaching about hell is for us to fear and change our own self-destructive tendencies and ways we judge, stigmatize, and destroy each other. Some of those infected with and affected by HIV/AIDS know firsthand in their own bodies that this affliction is a result of things they did or did not do; others are innocent victims infected in their mother's womb. Almost everyone who bears this dread disease suffers from rejection by others.

For example, one of the counselors we met in South Africa told us her story. She grew up in abusive circumstances with an aunt and uncle, became pregnant while at university, then discovered she was HIV-positive. Her baby died of AIDS in less than two years. After many experiences of being stigmatized and judged, she finally found a healing community in a church and trained as a counselor to work with AIDS sufferers. "God was able to forgive me, but it was hard to forgive myself," she says. "What I needed from the church was acceptance, love and hope, not judgment."

One is reminded of the gospel story of the man born blind told in John 9. When asked, "Who sinned, this man or his parents?" "Neither," says Jesus, "but this happened so that the work of God might be displayed in his life." (John 9:7). So God's work might be displayed, maybe more of us need to learn from Jesus how "to descend into another's hell" (p. 108) and thus display the work of God in our lives. We are called to bring the Light of the World and the grace of Jesus to those caught in the darkness and despair of hell, whether that hell is of their own making or the evildoing of others. There may be judgment in the hell of AIDS. There may be judgment in attacks against ordinary Americans or indiscriminate bombing of innocent civilians to bring terrorists to justice. These are hardly the kinds of judgment God brings, however, but hells we must enter with God's light. Amid such ongoing complexities and traumas, perhaps Klassen can be encouraged to write another book about what the Bible says about judgment and how God's judgment is and is not expressed in the pain humans inflict on each other.

Nevertheless, the book remains both a rich resource and a source of fruitful questions. Even as Klassen has masterfully presented the biblical texts about hell and outlined clearly his own theological position, questions about what happens to those who have never heard of Jesus, and how missionary zeal will be affected if there is no hell, will continue to trouble us. At the same time, when one is no longer motivated by fear, one can begin to experience heaven *on earth* as well as the darker side of life, which we humans know and experience all too often. If it is really true that "no judgment passage asks anything about the doctrines or beliefs of the individual!" and that "*all* judgment passages refer to our deeds, not to our profession of faith," then maybe there are better ways to engage in dialogue persons who follow other world religions and more effective ways to back up with deeds and actions our efforts at mission and evangelistic preaching.

Certainly, as Klassen so eloquently emphasizes, the God revealed in Jesus is a God of generosity, grace, and love. Several years ago I was greatly blessed by a sermon Laura Schmidt preached about the parable of the wheat and weeds (Matt. 13:24-30, 36-43).[3] Among other things she says that this parable makes it clear that both good and evil exist, but we are not the reapers.

Our knowledge of good and evil is never deep enough to purge another from the kingdom. Only God sees that clearly . . . the judgment of who's in and who's out of the kingdom is not up to us. . . . We can trust in God's just judgment of good and evil in the end. . . . The challenge for us is living in the time between sowing and harvest, in the time of wheat and weeds, in the world and in the church. God grant us wisdom, that we may extend mercy to each other as we grow. (p. 101)

Klassen has done a good job of letting the weeds and the wheat grow together in his readers' minds. Without forcing a certain position, he has been clear about how he personally experiences a grace-filled God, whose judgment always has the intent of helping us follow him more closely.

The beauty of Klassen's thinking, preaching, and writing seems to me to be his clear statement of faith in a good God who wants to shower his grace on both the good and the evil. Does this mean God condones evil? Or that evil will win in the end? By no means!

For I am convinced that neither death nor life, neither angels nor demons, neither the present nor the future, nor any powers, neither height nor depth, nor anything else in all creation, will be able to separate us from the love of God that is in Christ Jesus our Lord. (Rom. 8:37-39 NIV)

—*Delores Friesen, Ph.D., MFT (marriage and family therapist), Fresno, California, is Associate Professor of Pastoral Counseling, Mennonite Brethren Biblical Seminary.*

The Prosecutor Is Missing

Randy Klassen is to be commended for writing this book and Pandora Press U.S. for publishing it. It is never easy to swim against the stream. When the topic is as loaded as this one, when it challenges long-held conservative theological positions, to say that hell does not exist in the traditionally held view is tantamount to heresy. In the sixteenth century they would have burned both author and publisher; today many Christians merely raise their eyebrows.

It seems to me that a good place to start thinking about hell is to recognize that nobody has been there and come back to give an eyewitness first-hand report. That doesn't mean it's all made up, pure imagination. Indeed not. What it does give is a very necessary perspective.

Even a brief review of the history of hell raises questions. For instance, in Norse mythology hell was not hot but freezing cold. For ancient Jews, *Sheol*, usually translated "hell," was a cavern in the center of the earth for keeping the dead. They were a miserable lot, not fully conscious, kept in total darkness, and deprived of any joy of living. But their hell did not consist of brimstone and fire. All that came later.

In the fourth century, Augustine, Archbishop of Hippo, was probably the first Christian to expound at length and in great detail the doctrine of eternal punishment. Since he was considered an academic authority and a giant on spiritual matters, the church accepted his teaching and from time to time embellished it. Hell really got hot.

Some years ago a visiting evangelist in our church followed the example of the well-known preacher, Jonathan Edwards, of the mid-seventeen hundreds, and used fear of hell as a means to scare the kids into accepting Christ. Several times he said, "Where will you be tomorrow, if you die tonight?"

Finally our fourteen-year-old daughter raised her hand and replied, "We'll probably wake up right here in Akron, Pennsylvania. Wouldn't the better question be, 'Whom will we serve when we wake up tomorrow?'" Needless to say, we were proud of her.

What Randy Klassen has done so well is examine carefully all significant references to hell in the Old and New Testaments and shown that none provides clear evidence of the existence of hell as a place of eternal punishment.

Most convincing of all is his frequent reference to the character and teaching of Jesus, and how these simply do not resonate nor harmonize with the prevailing views of hell. He says that "Jesus revealed a love and grace in God unparalleled in any religion or philosophy." Hell, on the other hand, is a place where sinners are condemned to suffer the most inhuman pain for all eternity. There doesn't seem to be any love or compassion. Not even justice.

Part of the problem arises from a literal interpretation of the Bible. Klassen addresses this in a delightful and convincing chapter, showing that even Jesus sometimes spoke in allegorical, metaphorical, and hyperbolic language.

All this, however, does not mean that there will be no consequences to our actions. With freedom comes responsibility. God created us free beings, we can choose to love and serve him, or we can defy him and nail Jesus to the cross. That raises the question of a final judgment. Klassen is right in focusing on this. He does it in chapter 5, "Judgment in the Epistles," and again in chapter 9, "Criteria of Judgment." Klassen says, "Judgment is taught" (in the Bible). And again: "I cannot dilute the seriousness of judgment." That's good.

In fact it's so good that I would like to express thoughts on the final day of judgment beyond those in the book. Imagine for a moment that we have died and are in the courtroom in the Great Beyond. Our day of judgment has come. There, as here on earth, is a judge (God), a prosecutor (Satan or the Devil), a defense lawyer (Jesus), and the defendant, or accused (that's me). I know, even before the proceedings begin, that I am guilty. I have done what I should not have done, and have left undone what I should have done.

I also know the prosecutor is the one I need to fear. He's got it in for me. He's able and clever, he knows all the tricks of the trade. He can twist our words like a cord. He's brilliant and mean. In fact, he's a liar. Jesus said, "When he [Satan] speaks, he speaks according to his own nature, for he is a liar and the father of lies" (John 8:44). While we were still on earth he told us that going to war would bring peace, that alcohol and drugs would make us happy, possessions and wealth would satisfy all our longings, and more garbage like that.

However, now I'm not on earth. I've crossed the Jordan; I'm in the courtroom of God. I tremble, because I know the prosecutor will be playing no games, he's playing for keeps.

He wants me in his kingdom. If I plead the blood of Christ, that Jesus died for my sins, he'll prove in no time flat that I have a second-hand faith. A faith handed down to me by my parents and the church. It's not genuinely mine. It's fake. I'm a hypocrite.

But wait. That's how he troubled me on earth. That's how it was before Good Friday. We may not understand what happened when Jesus cried out from the cross, "It is finished!" but the Bible tells us enough to take away all fear and make us rejoice.

It says that "In dying he [Jesus] broke the power of the devil who had the power of death" (Heb.2:14). And again: "The reason the son of God appeared was to destroy the works of the devil" (1. John 3:8). Or just listen to this: "The accuser of our brethren has been thrown down, who accuses them day and night before God" (Rev.12:10). Get that! He's been thrown down! My prosecutor has been thrown down!

So now let's take another look at the courtroom. God is there. Jesus is there. I am there, "guilty as hell"—and that's not using bad language. And over there is the chair of the prosecutor. It's empty. What happened? Is he late? More than anything else I wish to be spared prosecution. But is my rising hope based on an illusion?

Indeed not! It's real. He's not there, and he's not coming. He knows his game is up.

He knows what happened on Good Friday and on the day of Resurrection. He knows he has no hold on the person who has said "YES" to Jesus Christ and accepted him as his Lord and Savior. John says, "Blessed are the dead who die in the Lord" (Rev.14:13). Jesus said, "He who hears my word and believes him who sent me, has eternal life; he does *not* come into judgment, but has passed from death to life" (John 5:24, emph. added). Paul wrote to the Romans, "There is therefore now no condemnation for those who are in Jesus Christ" (Rom. 8:1).

Almost too good to be true. But that is the bottom line about the judgment. There will be no interrogation or cross-examination for those who are "in Christ," because the prosecutor failed to show up. The divine computer with its instant replay of my entire life is blank.

God, our creator, is there. He has always loved us, as Jesus portrayed it in the story of the Prodigal Son. (Luke 15). Jesus is there who gave his life for us. This is the good news of the Bible. No, I'm not innocent; Jesus my Savior covered for me. Hallelujah!

Listen carefully:

> What then shall we say to this? If God is for us, who is against us? He who did not spare his own Son but gave him up for us all, will he not also give us all things with him? Who shall bring any charge against God's elect? It is God who justifies; who is to condemn? It is Christ Jesus, who died, yes, who was raised from the dead, who is at the right hand of God, who indeed intercedes for us! (Rom. 8:31-34)

That, I believe, is the bottom line. Hallelujah!

What God will do with those who heard the Word but did not believe, or with those millions who never heard the good news, I don't know. I think nobody knows. God, the all-wise, the loving and caring Creator, will take care of them.

> But I know whom I have believed,
> and am persuaded
> that He is able.
> To keep that which I've committed,
> Unto Him against that day.

—Peter J. Dyck, Scottdale, Pennsylvania, is in active retirement, speaking and writing. His latest and sixth book is Getting Home Before Dark *(Herald Press, 2001).*

Guidelines for Discussion

AS THIS BOOK DOCUMENTS, LIKE MANY OTHER pastors and teachers of the Christian faith, I have felt a growing uneasiness about the traditional doctrine of hell. Yet it seemed to be what the Bible was saying. "Have we understood the Bible correctly?" became my question.

I began this study with no preconceived conclusions in mind. For this reason, in an effort to maintain at least some objectivity, I have made reference in my book to each significant biblical reference to hell, as well as to the major teachings on judgment. It was then my intention to harmonize these insights on hell with the character of God as revealed in Jesus Christ. Here is where my questions arose. This prompted answers in a direction different than the traditional view.

I expect there will be no argument against understanding the divine purpose of judgment as being to lead to repentance. Where fellow believers will challenge me will be in my suggestion that God's purpose in judgment does not necessarily cease for us when we die. To suggest that sinners may have a "second chance" after death has often been labeled heretical.

My response is to ask, "Does God cease to be gracious after the time of his children's death"? Why should the judgment of God stop convicting those who have heretofore rejected his love? Is not such patience and mercy more consistent with the character of God than an immediate shut-down of opportunity at the time of death?

This becomes especially germane when we remember that most people on earth have never heard of the grace of God in Jesus Christ. If Jesus is the only means of salvation, could there not be a meeting with him after this life is over for those who never met him before? I only pose the questions. I offer no definitive answers. But clearly I do lean in the direction of "amazing grace."

Another challenge to my position will come from those who fear such teaching will diminish evangelistic zeal and dull the whole missionary enterprise. My response is that the opposite will be true. I would far rather proclaim the God whom Jesus describes in his parables, in Luke 15, for example, than a God who is the perpetrator of an endless holocaust. The early disciples were wonderfully effective in preaching and demonstrating the good news of God's amazing love without threats of hell. Recall chapter 2 on "Apostolic Preaching."

Healthy discussion can focus on these issues as broken down into a number of questions which follow. Certainly if true discussion and discernment is to ensue, groups must be free to disagree with my conclusions. However, my hope is that discussion leaders will also aim to give the perspectives presented in this book an adequate hearing. I suggest that this will involve making sure to keep the big picture big—that is, to allow no verse here or there too quickly to invalidate the big picture of God as the loving heavenly Parent of all people, as Jesus revealed.

The tension between God's love and holiness, between mercy and justice must be maintained. Heaven and hell are both realities taught in our Scriptures, but they must be understood in a manner consistent with the revelation of God as seen in the life and witness of Jesus Christ. Wrestling with that tension has been a key goal of this book and I hope can likewise be a goal of any discussions.

For Pastors

I hope some of the material gathered in this book will provide inspiration and illustration for fellow pastors. While I am not necessarily urging sermons on hell, the judgment theme is inevitable in preaching from Scripture. I am hoping some of my research will prove helpful in preparing strong sermons.

For Groups

The best forum for a healthy discussion of this topic is the small group. While I have enjoyed some profitable discussion in groups of up to thirty or forty participants, the best opportunity for fruitful discussion usually happens in smaller groups of between ten and fourteen or less. The leader needs to be the most familiar with the contents of my book but must also allow for sharing of all opinions. The challenge to the group will be to check every viewpoint as to its consistency with the light of Christ.

Using the following questions can make for a healthy Sunday school class series for adults, college students, or senior high age.

Questions for Discussion

1. Faithfulness to biblical teaching is required of all Christians. The Bible does teach a message on hell. However, the doctrine of hell as a place of eternal conscious torment of the lost may need to be re-examined. Is this what the Bible is actually saying? If so, or if not, what is the concept or purpose of a message on hell? See Matthew 25: 41-46

2. If the theme of hell as a place of endless suffering is largely absent from first-century proclamation, what does that tell us about the early disciples understanding of Jesus' references to hell? Look at all the sermons and testimonies in the book of Acts.

3. Since the art of language includes a great variety of communication forms—narrative, poetry, metaphor, hyperbole, allegory, parable—it becomes crucial for us to learn the literary form of a text to properly interpret it. How do we go

about discerning what form our biblical text is taking? Compare Luke 6: 27-31 with Luke 16: 19-31.

4. What can we learn from church history, where we see the Christian community using the Bible to justify the Crusades, anti-Semitism, slavery, the subjugation of women, and other follies which today the church rejects?

5. How do these historical happenings challenge us in our interpretations of hell? Could our sinful desire for vengeance play a part in this?

6. If we believe God's love will ultimately prevail for all people, how do we maintain the key teaching of judgment (hell), namely the serious consequences of doing evil and rejecting God's grace? See John 5;28-28 and Romans 5: 18-19.

7. In our attempts at justice, we often say that "the punishment must fit the crime." If this is valid, could everlasting condemnation be justified for time-bound sins? In the Old Testament, limits on punishment were mandated. See Exodus 21:24-25.

8. When is the threat of consequences an appropriate message of love? Discuss several examples. See Galatians 6:7-8.

9. Some evangelists feel called to use the threat of hell as a motivating factor in winning converts. Discuss the strength or weakness of such an approach and compare your answers to "the great commission" in Matthew 28:19.

10. What view of judgment fits with the character, style and teaching of Jesus Christ? Look at Revelation 6:12-18.

11. How are we to understand inclusive passages such as Romans 14: 11-12: Philippians 2:10-11: 1, Peter 4:5-6?

12. Much of what happens to us after this life is over remains shrouded in mystery. But the promises for the children of God are full of hope while the destiny of unbelievers is dark. Regardless of the mercy God may yet show to those who do evil, why is it still much wiser to commit to God's way today than to put off following the Lord for even a day? See Hebrews 3:7-9 and Psalms 16:11.

13. Accommodating a doctrine to fit the culture is an ever-present temptation for the church. Was it not an accom-

modation to the culture that led the church to justify slavery? In that situation, the church often found biblical texts to support the prevailing view, but now we see the biblical message very differently. The same can be said about how the church understood the place and role of women. Is the view of hell in this book an accommodation to our culture or is it a clearer reading of the biblical revelation?

14. A rabbi friend once said the Holocaust was hell. There was no need to postulate another hell to come after this life. Why is it important to accept the biblical teaching that there is a time of accounting coming for all people after this life is over? Do the terrible injustices in our world cry out for a final resolution when the Judge of all the earth ultimately sets thing right? Meanwhile, is a primary task of Christian evangelism to eliminate the many hells people are experiencing today? Mother Teresa brought heaven into the hell-holes of Calcutta as she put into action Christ's love for the diseased and dying helpless ones. Should this be our calling? How do we balance emphasis on judgment beyond this life versus addressing hell in this life?

Notes

CHAPTER 1: PERSONAL PILGRIMAGE

1. Mary Baxter, *A Divine Revelation of Hell* (New Kensington, Pa.: Whitaker House,1993), 95.

2. Ibid., 213.

3. Jan Bonda, *The One Purpose of God* (Grand Rapids, Mich.: William B. Eerdmans Publishing Co., English trans. 1998).

CHAPTER 2: APOSTOLIC PREACHING

1. Richard Longenecker, *Biblical Exegesis in the Apostolic Period* (Grand Rapids: William B. Eeerdmans, 1975), 83.

2. Robert A. Peterson, *Hell on Trial* (Phillipsburg, N.J.: P. and R. Publishing, 1995), 77-96.

CHAPTER 3: NO HELL IN THE OLD TESTAMENT

1. Stuart E. Rosenberg, *The Christian Problem* (New York: Hippocrene Books, 1986), 36.

2. Abraham Heschel, *The Prophets* (New York: Harper & Row Publishers, 1962), 286.

3. Ibid., 291.

4. Peterson, 34.

5. John Goldingay, *Daniel, World Biblical Commentary*, vol. 3 (Word Publishing, Dallas: 1989), 306.

6. Ibid., 308.

7. Ibid., 319.

8. Bonda, 212.

9. Ibid., 219.

10. Rosenberg, 37.

11. John Walvoord, "The Literal View," in *Four Views on Hell*, ed. William V. Crockett (Grand Rapids: Zondervan Publishing House, 1996), 17.

12. Leon Klenecki, Richard John Neuhaus, *Believing Today: Jew and Christian in Conversation* (Grand Rapids: William B. Eeerdmans: 1989), 33.

13. Walvoord, 17.

14. Alan E. Bernstein, *The Foundation of Hell* (Ithaca, N.Y.: Cornell University Press, 1998), 176.

15. Jaroslav Pelikan, *The Shape of Death; Life Death and Immortality in the Early Fathers* (New York: Abington Press, 1961).

CHAPTER 4: HELL IN THE GOSPELS

1. Leon Morris, "The Dreadful Harvest," *Christianity Today* (May 27, 1991), 34.

2. William Barclay, *The Gospel of Matthew, Daily Study Bible Series*, vol. 1 (Philadelphia: Westminster Press), 141.

3. Robert Guelich, *The Sermon on the Mount* (Dallas: Word Publishing, 1982), 188.

4. Bonda, *The One Purpose of God*.

5. Ibid., 214.

CHAPTER 5: JUDGMENT IN THE EPISTLES

1. Peterson, 77.

2. Bernstein, 176.

3. John R. W. Stott, "Basic Stott," *Christianity Today* (Jan. 8, 1996), 28.

4. Bonda, 213.

CHAPTER 6: ORIGINS OF BELIEF IN HELL

1. Andrew Wilson, ed., *World Scripture: A Comparative Anthology of Sacred Texts* (St. Paul, Minn.: Paragon House, 1991), 246.

2. Alice Turner, *The History of Hell* (San Diego: Harcourt Brace and Company, A Harvest Book, 1993), 3.

3. Augustine, "On the Sacraments of the Christian Faith" 2.18, in *Four Views on Hell*. ed. William V. Crockett, 155.

4. William V. Crockett, *Four Views on Hell*, 47.

5. Here Crockett is quoting Saul Liebermen, in *Text and Studies* (New York: KTAV, 1974), 29-56.

6. *Eerdman's Handbook to The History of Christianity* (Carmel, N.Y.: Guideposts, 1977), 198.

7. John Paul II made these comments July 28, 1999, during his weekly address to the audience at the Vatican.

8. *The Baptist Faith and Message* (adopted by the Southern Baptist Convention, May 9, 1963), 15.

9. Bruce Bauer, *Stealing Jesus* (New York: Crown Publishers, Inc., 1997), 211.

10. Jim Hill and Rod Cheadle, *The Bible Tells Me So* (New York: Anchor Books, Doubleday, 1996), 4.

11. Ibid., 4.

12. Clark Pinnock, "The Conditional View," in *Four Views on Hell*, ed. William V. Crockett, 140.

13. John R. W. Stott, "Basic Stott," 28.

14. Ramesh P. Richard, *The Population of Heaven* (Chicago: Moody Press, 1994).

CHAPTER 7:
THE PROBLEM OF A LITERALISTIC INTERPRETATION

1. Timothy George, "What We Mean When We Say It's True," *Christianity Today* (October 23, 1995).

2. Donald A. Hagner, "The New Testament Criticism," *Theology News and Notes* (Pasadena, Calif.: A Publication of Fuller Theological Seminary, June 1998), 7.

3. John Blanchard, *Whatever Happened to Hell?* (Wheaton, Ill.: Crossway Books, 1995).

4. Jerry Falwell, *Finding Inner Peace and Strength*, 26, quoted in John Shelby Spong, *Rescuing the Bible from Fundamentalism* (San Francisco: HarperSanFrancisco, 1991), 25.

5. W. A. Criswell, *Why I Preach That The Bible Is Literally True* (Nashville: Broadman Publishers, 1995), 99.

6. John Shelby Spong, *Rescuing the Bible from Fundamentalism* (San Francisco: Harper, 1991).

CHAPTER 8:
REJECTING THE TRADITIONAL VIEW OF HELL

1. Crockett, "The Metaphorical View," *Four Views on Hell*.

2. John R. W. Stott, David Edwards, *Essentials: A Liberal Evangelical Dialogue* (London: Hadden & Stoughton, 1988), 314.

3. Clark H. Pinnock, Robert C. Brow, *Unbounded Love* (Downers Grove, Ill.: Intervarsity Press, 1994).

4. Pinnock, "The Conditional View," 140.

5. Edward G. Selwyn, *The First Epistle of Peter* (London: Macmillan, 1961), 358.

6. Pinnock, "The Conditional View," 148.

7. Ibid., 149.

8. Philip Yancey, *What's So Amazing About Grace* (Grand Rapids: Zondervan Publishing House, 1997).

9. Bonda, 29.

10. Pinnock, "The Conditional View," 149.

11. Hans Küng, *Eternal Life: Life After Death as a Medical, Philosophical, and Theological Problem* (New York: Doubleday, 1984), 136.

12. Thomas Aquinas, *Summa Theologies* (Suppl. Q. 94).

13. John R. W. Stott, *Essentials: A Liberal Evangelical Dialogue*, 319.

14. Leslie D. Weatherhead, *The Christian Agnostic* (Nashville, Tenn.: Abington, 1965), 285.

CHAPTER 9: CRITERIA OF JUDGMENT

1. Klyne Snodgrass, *Between Two Truths* (Grand Rapids: Zondervan Publishing House, 1990), 95.

2. Barna Research Group, "Christians Are More Likely to Experience Divorce than Are Non-Christians" (December 21, 1999), accessed at http://www.barna.org.

3. Leon Morris, "The Dreadful Harvest," *Christianity Today* (May 27, 1991), 37.

4. Erwin W. Lutzer, *One Minute After You Die* (Chicago, Ill.: Moody Press, 1977), 101.

5. Robert Short, *Short Meditations on the Bible and Peanuts* (Louisville, Ky.: Westminster/John Knox Press, 1990), 127.

CHAPTER 10: ABOUT THE ULTIMATE FUTURE

1. William Barclay, *The Letters of James and Peter* (Philadelphia.: The Westminster Press, 1960), 295.

2. Eugene Peterson, *Under the Unpredictable Plant* (Grand Rapids: William B. Eeerdmans, 1992), 95.

3. Jeffrey Burton Russell, *Satan* (Ithaca, N.Y.: Cornell University Press, 1981), 122.

4. Frederick Buechner, *Whistling in the Dark* (San Francisco: HarperSan Francisco, HarperCollins Publishers, 1993), 39-40.

5. Elton Trueblood, *The Humor of Christ* (New York and London, Harper & Row Publishers, 1964), 32, 140.

6. Heschel, 282, 286.

7. Short, 129.

8. William Barclay, *A Spiritual Autobiography* (Grand Rapids: William B. Eeerdmans, 1995), 58.

9. Snodgrass, 114.

CHAPTER 11: RESPONSES

1. Sandra M. Schneiders, *The Revelatory Text: Interpreting the New Testament as Sacred Scripture* (Collegeville, Minn.: The Liturgical Press, 1999), 144.

2. Ibid., 165.

3. Published in *All Are Witnesses*, ed. Delores Friesen (Kindred Press, 1996), 97-101.

The Author

*R*ANDY KLASSEN WAS BORN IN Winnipeg, Manitoba, Canada. With his family, he attended a Mennonite Brethren Church where, after his conversion, he was baptized. His commitment to Christ and call to ministry came largely through contact with InterVarsity Christian Fellowship while at University of Manitoba. From there, he attended Fuller Theological Seminary for two years.

Not being a citizen of the United States and running short of money, he returned to Winnipeg, where he was surprised by a call to serve as interim pastor of Teien Covenant Church in Drayton, North Dakota. After eighteen months there, he completed his theological training at North Park Theological Seminary in 1959.

During the next forty years, Klassen served Covenant churches in Winnipeg, Canada; Davis, California; Prairie Village, Kansas; Valley Springs, California; and Chandler, Arizona. From 1977-81, he served as the Executive Secretary of Evangelism for the Covenant Church.

At the end of this term, he stepped out of official ministerial duties to pursue what was to be an increasingly successful art career. However, during this time, he continued to lead home Bible studies. One Bible study in Valley Springs grew into Good Samaritan Community Covenant Church, and Randy was officially back into the ministry. He remained there for eight years, until he was called to serve Hope Covenant Church in Chandler, from which he retired in 1999.

At that point, Klassen and his wife, Joyce, returned to their favorite region, the "Mother Lode" area of northern California, where they now live in the town of San Andreas. Randy continues to do pulpit supply on Sundays, still does home Bible studies, participates in a part-time care ministry to other pastors, paints watercolors, walks his Dalmatian, and yes, also likes to write.

Printed in the United States
201133BV00001B/1-30/A